LONG SHADOWS

LONG SHADOWS

The Farewell to JFK

JIM LEEKE

Attic Window Publishing, Inc.
Alexandria, VA

Attic Window Publishing, Inc., Alexandria, VA 22304

Printed in the United States of America
12 11 10 09 08   1 2 3 4 5

Library of Congress Control Number: 2007940598

ISBN-13: 978-0-9722274-2-1
ISBN-10: 0-9722274-2-3

Design and layout by Vincent Hughes, Visualization

Front cover: Caisson bearing the president's casket leaving the White House for the Capitol, Sunday, November 24, 1963.

Back cover: Robert Kennedy and Jacqueline Kennedy departing the burial services at Arlington National Cemetery, Monday, November 25, 1963.

Photo credits: By Ollie Atkins, courtesy Special Collections and Archives, George Mason University Libraries, p. 77; by Abbie Rowe, National Park Service, courtesy of John F. Kennedy Presidential Library and Museum, pp. 37, 53, 65, 107; by Abbie Rowe, National Park Service, courtesy of Harry S. Truman Library, pp. 90, 95, 114, back cover; by Cecil Stoughton, courtesy Lyndon Baines Johnson Library and Museum, p. 16; courtesy of John F. Kennedy Presidential Library and Museum, cover, pp. 18, 31, 99; courtesy of The Old Guard Museum, Ft. Myer, Virginia, pp. 60, 101, 104; courtesy of U.S. Army Band, pp. 113, 57. Author photo by Jaime Santillan, courtesy of Jim Leeke.

Diagrams adapted by Vincent Hughes, Visualization, from Mossman, B. C., and M. W. Stark. *The Last Salute: Civil and Military Funerals, 1921–1969.* Washington, 1991.

For my wife,
Jane C. Clark,
with love.

And to the memory of
Tere Rios Versace,
at peace in Arlington.

Ceremony is man's built-in reaction to tragedy.

— Charles Collingwood,
CBS News

Up ahead General Wehle heard "only the drums, the terrible drums" . . .

— William Manchester,
The Death of a President

Of John Fitzgerald Kennedy's funeral it can be said he would have liked it.

— Mary McGrory,
Washington Evening Star

Contents

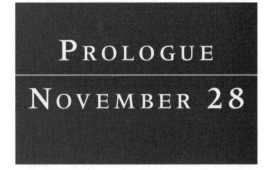

PROLOGUE
NOVEMBER 28

THURSDAY, NOVEMBER 28
THANKSGIVING DAY

PROLOGUE

Lieutenant Eugene H. Bickley, an army radio and television officer, reported early Thanksgiving morning for special duty amid the autumn-brown hills of Arlington National Cemetery. Visitors were already gathering at the gates, across Memorial Bridge from downtown Washington. Bickley stood watching from a tarpaulin covering the wet ground near President Kennedy's gravesite.

Fifteen thousand people would pay their respects here today, all that the site and line would accommodate. They were a fraction of all who would come—two hundred thousand altogether, more than any other day in Arlington's history, about a tenth of the area's population. Few were weeping. But people were drained and Bickley did not see a single smiling face among them.

The lieutenant had been here three days ago, that bright, terrible Monday, helping the hundreds of print and broadcast journalists covering the president's funeral. Tears had streaked Bickley's face as he drove out through the gates afterward. Today felt different, a strange holiday that *The Washington Post* later called mournful and bleak. Visitors kept arriving during the morning until the narrow roads through the cemetery became gridlocked.

Captain Michael D. Groves, from the army's Third U.S. Infantry regiment, joined Bickley on the tarpaulin. Groves was "tall, broad-shouldered, and tough," Bickley thought, a strict officer who always tried to do his job perfectly. Today, the captain looked haggard and wan. Bickley asked how he was feeling.

Before Groves could reply, First Lieutenant Samuel R. Bird stepped up and saluted. He and Groves served in the Third Infantry's elite honor guard company, the unit responsible for state and military funerals and other important ceremonies. Bird had led the escort for the late president's casket. Groves was his company commander.

Neither man wore a West Point class ring. Groves had graduated from Eastern Michigan College near Detroit, Bird from the Citadel, a prestigious military school in Charleston, South Carolina. They were ambitious officers, each eager to leave spit-and-polish Washington for the brushfire war in South Vietnam. A month earlier, enemy Viet Cong forces had captured a former Third Infantry officer, now listed as missing.

"You sure look beat, sir," Bird said to his captain. "When did you last sleep?"

Groves returned Bird's salute with a weak smile.

"I don't remember, Sam, but I will this weekend," he said. "I've got a three-day pass starting tomorrow." Groves badly needed the time away. In addition to the stress of his duties, his wife, Mary Frances, was eight months pregnant with their second child. Even a twenty-seven-year-old infantry commander had limitations.

Groves soon left the gravesite to speak to soldiers coming on duty. Bird stepped away for a word with a sergeant. Bickley stood alone, watching the visitors quietly filing past the president's grave. *The Washington Post* called the mound inside a white picket fence "the Nation's newest and saddest shrine."

VIPs arrived periodically throughout the morning. Senator Edward Kennedy and his wife, Joan. Actor Peter Lawford and his wife, Pat, the late president's sister. Others, including the mayor of San Francisco. Ordinary people paused to give them privacy, then again moved quietly past the grave. The weather was dreary and cold. Shortly before noon, the crowd murmured. Bickley looked down the long slope to see Jacqueline Kennedy stepping from a limousine.

The former first lady walked up the hill, composed and somber, accompanied by aides, secret service agents and her sister, Princess Lee Radziwill. Mrs. Kennedy had planned or requested many of the finest moments of her husband's funeral. Her grace amid sorrow seemed to embody his New Frontier ideals. Bickley had stood a few yards from her in the Capitol rotunda on Sunday and come to admire "this marvelous woman's dignity."

The visit today was Mrs. Kennedy's fifth to the grave since the funeral. This afternoon, the *Washington Daily News* would run a prominent photo of her dressed all in black but smiling behind dark glasses, as if to reassure its readers she had survived her ordeal. She stopped at the grave and knelt to pray. For several minutes, Bickley didn't hear a sound in the vast cemetery. When she rose, she walked farther up the slope to gaze at row upon row of flowers placed in her husband's memory. Then she turned to take in the magnificent view of the city across the Potomac.

"Even in her grief," Bickley recalled, "she stopped and spoke in muted tones to several people. She nodded, sighed and turned back down the hill. The crowds grew close, almost engulfing her."

Mrs. Kennedy recognized Lieutenant Bird and paused to thank him for all he had done. Then agents cleared a path back toward her car. She stumbled slightly descending the slope, as she had the afternoon of the burial. Bickley reached out with another officer to take her arms. "Please make way for Mrs. Kennedy," they pleaded. The visitors obediently stepped aside to form a lane to the limousine.

There wasn't anything left for Bickley or anyone to say to her. Less than a week had passed since Air Force One had brought Mrs. Kennedy back from Dallas. She was no longer their first lady. Lyndon Johnson was the president. At Andrews Air Force Base in Maryland, another air force plane waited to take her and the children home to Massachusetts.

As her car slowly pulled away, Lieutenant Bickley saluted.

FRIDAY
NOVEMBER 22

ANDREWS

M ost of uniformed Washing-ton learned that shots had been fired at the president in Dallas at one-thirty, eastern standard time, in the same way that civilians did. Someone heard a terse news bulletin, rushed to tell someone else, and soon everyone was clustered around a radio or television set.

Sergeant Robert Gill was a twenty-one-year-old marine from Cape Cod who was kidded in the White House honor guard for sounding so much like one of the Kennedys. Gill was packing for a weekend in New York City when liberty was abruptly canceled. "You're not going anywhere," he and his buddies were told. "The president has been shot."

Lieutenant Sam Bird had marched in the president's inaugural parade in 1961 as a Citadel cadet. Although a conservative Kansas republican, he felt an affinity for his commander-in-chief. Today, Bird had worked a funeral at Arlington for an elderly colonel and returned to Fort Myer, the tidy old post behind the cemetery. Like Gill, he heard someone say the president had been shot.

"Oh, really," Bird replied. He took two steps before it registered. "The *who*?"

First Lieutenant Richard A. Lipsey lived across the hall from Bird in Fort Myer's bachelor officers' quarters. His boss was Major General Philip C. Wehle (pronounced "Wheel"), the commander of the Military District of Washington, known by the acronym MDW. The army district had been formed in World War II to plan a ground defense of the capital.

Entitled to two aides, General Wehle preferred just one, efficient, twenty-four-year-old Lipsey. The lieutenant was driving to pick up the general when a bulletin came over the radio. Wehle heard the same news at his home. They met at the general's front door.

"I was coming in as he was coming out," Lipsey remembered. "We went immediately back to our office and got on the phone with the White House. Got on the phone with the Pentagon. Got on the phone with everybody else."

One of the people Wehle contacted was Paul C. Miller, MDW chief of ceremonies. Miller was a lean and leathery retired army lieutenant colonel, born to missionaries in China but reared in Nebraska. He had earned a silver star and purple heart in World War II before being captured by Germans in Italy.

Miller's bible was a manual, *State, Official and Special Military Funeral Policies and Plans*. On learning of the president's death, Miller informed the White House that the Military District of Washington would be ready for whatever was required. This was an optimistic but ultimately accurate assessment.

Nationwide radio and television made the announcement shortly after two-thirty. Anchorman Walter Cronkite was live on the air for CBS News. "From Dallas, Texas, the flash, apparently official," he began, reading off a sheet of paper. "President Kennedy died at one p.m. Central

Standard Time, two o'clock Eastern Standard Time. Some thirty-eight minutes ago."

Lieutenant Bird was in his car at Fort Myer when he saw soldiers lowering the post's American flag to half-staff. He leapt out to salute.

Bird's unit, the Third Infantry, was called the "Old Guard" within the army and MDW. Based at Fort Myer since 1948, it was responsible for posting sentinels at the Tomb of the Unknowns at Arlington, conducting state and military funerals, and protecting key government buildings in a crisis. In military circles and official Washington, it was famous.

The army selected troops for the regiment based on their height, appearance, fitness and the likelihood of obtaining a security clearance (no man remained without one). Bird and his men in E Company wore the distinctive tab of the honor guard company. They rightly considered themselves special. Bird knew immediately that he and they would participate in services for the late president.

MDW was prepared to hold funerals for former presidents Herbert Hoover, Harry Truman and Dwight Eisenhower and for retired General of the Army Douglas MacArthur. An aircraft had been adapted to carry horses and a caisson to Missouri should Truman die suddenly. The Third Infantry had recently rehearsed a funeral for Hoover, who was still seriously ill in New York but no longer near death. But these plans were all for old men. Little in Miller's manual fit the younger thirty-fifth president. The Old Guard had never foreseen, an officer said, "that our practice was preparing us for President Kennedy."

General Wehle quickly opened MDW's funeral operations center, located in old wartime buildings at Gravelly Point, on the Virginia side of the Potomac just north of National Airport. The first task was to alert the military units and civil agencies likely to participate in services for the president. This included obtaining permission to use the U.S. Capitol in anticipation that the body would lie in state in the rotunda.

Ceremonies chief Paul Miller went to the White House that afternoon to see Sargent Shriver, who was both the Peace Corps director and the late president's brother-in-law. With special assistant Ralph A. Dungan, they began what army historians B. C. Mossman and M. W. Stark later termed "the difficult task of arranging funeral ceremonies under the pressure of time and without direct contact with the immediate family."

"Military officers in charge of state funerals are already in action," David Brinkley of NBC News told the nation shortly before four o'clock. "We assume that the army will be in charge of details."

The Old Guard didn't wait for official notification. Boots and shoes were shined, buckles buffed, uniforms pressed, equipment oiled and polished. The caisson platoon touched up paint, stripped harnesses and groomed the horses. The grimness of the Old Guard as it worked was more than strictly military.

"We were his own; we were the best," one soldier said long afterward. "We were basically his personal honor guard. To lose your commander-in-chief that way . . ."

The president's plane, Air Force One, was already on the way back to Andrews Air Force Base, home of the executive air wing. Bird received orders to select a team of Old Guard enlisted men to handle the president's casket. Drilled to meet the military traditions and physical demands of the duty, such men were called body bearers.

Of the eight husky, dependable soldiers Bird chose, the one he would rely on most was Sergeant James L. Felder, a draftee from Sumter, South Carolina. A college graduate and civil rights activist before the army, Felder had advanced four ranks to sergeant in less than two years. He had participated in perhaps a thousand military funerals. Precise, strong and dedicated, he was a first-rate soldier. Felder's mission now was the most important of his career.

Captain Kenneth S. Pond, the Third Infantry adjutant, arranged for a helicopter to fly Bird's casket team to meet the president's plane at Andrews.

Another Old Guard team headed for Joseph Gawler's Sons on Wisconsin Avenue, the most prestigious funeral home in Washington. These men were the "death watch," guards posted at the four corners of a casket under the eye of an officer. Such a guard for a fallen commander is an ancient military tradition. When president's body didn't arrive at Gawler's, the funeral home became a drill hall where the death watch honed its silent, slow-motion precision. Sergeant First Class James "Pete" Holder later concluded that his real mission was merely to decoy the press.

With momentous hours and days ahead, officers and sergeants in commands and military bands across Washington also began preparations. The U.S. Army Band at Fort Myer looked to its instruments and sheet music. The Old Guard Fife and Drum Corps went on alert, recalling everyone who was not on the post. The Air Force Pipe Band with its colorful "Billy Mitchell" tartans was in New Orleans, preparing for an evening performance. The pipe major got a call ordering the band's immediate return. The airmen packed their bags, left the navy barracks where they were quartered and headed back to Washington.

The armed forces weren't the only uniformed presence in the capital. The DC metropolitan police, too, responded rapidly to the news from Dallas. Chief Robert V. Murray kept his day shift on duty, along with the evening shift that reported at four o'clock. The additional officers were needed in part for traffic control as federal government workers went home early. A law student later remembered a traffic cop standing in tears as he directed cars and taxis through his intersection.

"Neither private nor Government offices officially closed, but they might as well have," the *Washington Daily News* reported. "The workers simply left. Where did everybody go?" To Chief Justice Earl Warren, it seemed that weekend "as though the world had stopped moving."

Other special-duty details fanned out across town. Police and secret service agents appeared shortly after three o'clock at the Capitol Hill office of Congressman John V. McCormack. The Massachusetts democrat was speaker of the house and next in line of succession to the presidency. McCormack accepted the protection, but quietly dismissed it within a few hours and went without until a new vice president was elected and sworn in more than a year later.

Secret service agents also arrived at The Elms, the Johnson family home on Fifty-second Street in northwest Washington; others in Texas guarded the elder daughter, Lynda Bird, a student at the university in Austin. Police began patrols as a crowd gathered across the street from the Johnsons', television trucks not far behind. Police also went to Lafayette Park opposite the White House, where more people had gathered. Both places remained somber and quiet.

Several installations in and around Washington were named for men killed in wartime—Bolling Air Force Base for Colonel Raynal C. Bolling, killed in France in 1918; Fort McNair for Lieutenant General Leslie J. McNair, killed by misdirected Allied bombs in France in 1944; Andrews for

Lieutenant General Frank M. Andrews, killed in an air crash in Iceland in 1943. If the names proved anything, it was that war was chaotic and savagely unpredictable.

As night fell, Andrews seemed to be at war. Arc lights harshly illuminated the tarmac and flight line. Secret service agents stood atop buildings and hangars. Senior members of the government clustered in silent groups. *The Times* of London called it "a nightmare scene."

The helicopter carrying Bird's casket team from Fort Myer landed at the base at five-thirty. With General Wehle also on the scene, a MDW captain told Lieutenant Bird to prepare for several contingencies for receiving the body when Air Force One arrived.

Honor guards and body bearers arrived from the other services, sent independently by their commands in case they were needed. Bird began assembling two joint-service casket teams, each with six men. He planned to have one team convey the president's casket from the plane to the tarmac and the other to carry it to the waiting transport. From the troops left over, Bird also created an eight-man army-air force team to form an honor cordon to President Johnson's helicopter.

Although hastily assembled, one of Bird's joint-service casket teams would remain together through the president's funeral. This included Sergeant Felder and Specialist Fourth Class Douglas A. Mayfield of the Old Guard; Staff Sergeant Richard E. Gaudreau of the air force; marine Lance Corporal Timothy F. Cheek; navy Seaman Apprentice Hubert Clark; and coast guard Yeoman Second Class George A. Barnum. Gaudreau and Barnum were equal in rank to Felder, but the Old Guard sergeant remained the noncommissioned officer in charge.

By dusk, about three thousand people, service personnel and families, stood along the fences at Andrews. More press had gathered than ever before or since. "I don't like this," a reporter said as they waited for Air Force One. "I don't want to write about this." George Tames, a veteran *New York Times* photographer who had known and liked the president, felt "sorry for myself and for the world."

The president's plane was a VC-137C Stratoliner, a well-appointed military version of the civilian Boeing 707. Pilot James B. Swindal was monitoring the secret service radio at Love Field in Dallas when he heard the first staccato reports from the motorcade.

Colonel Swindal had immediately prepared the plane to rush the president back to Walter Reed army hospital in Washington. "We hoped it was a wound," he recalled later. That hope died with the president.

Secret service agents hustled Lyndon Johnson and his wife from Parkland Hospital out to Love Field and the safety of the plane. Among the agents was Rufus Youngblood, who had shielded the vice president with his body during the shooting. He and Clint Hill, the agent who scrambled over the trunk of the president's limousine to reach Mrs. Kennedy, later received medals for their actions in Dallas. Youngblood took precautions now against the possibility of a second sniper at Love Field.

Marie Fehmer, a young Johnson secretary, remembered Youngblood "going through the plane and ordering everyone to slam those shades down. He was mean, he was cruel, he was yelling at us, and I didn't know what was going on."

Colonel Swindal left the plane to salute as the president's body arrived in a hearse about two-fifteen, Texas time. No thought was given to placing the casket in the baggage hold. Agents, aides and members of the flight crew carried it up a long ramp into the rear of the plane, which hadn't been designed for taking on cargo. The job was difficult and without ceremony. The chief flight engineer would always remember the vice president "helping us load the casket."

The crew lashed down the casket with straps in a sort of family living room at the rear of the plane; crewmen had hurriedly removed four seats and part of a bulkhead to make the space. Mrs. Kennedy had accompanied her husband's body in the hearse and now retired to an adjacent living compartment. Once airborne, she would sit beside her husband's casket during the entire flight back to Washington.

Nicholas Katzenbach, Robert Kennedy's deputy attorney general in Washington, dictated the presidential oath of office over the phone to Fehmer. At two thirty-six, central time, federal Judge Sarah T. Hughes used the secretary's typed notes for the swearing-in. The oath was a formality, since the vice president had ascended to the higher office the moment John Kennedy expired.

The ceremony in the hot, crowded cabin took two minutes. President Johnson then said, "Now, let's get airborne."

One of two pool reporters on board, Merriman Smith of United Press International, described Air Force One as "a big gleaming silver-and-blue fan-jet." Pilot Swindal lifted it off the runway at two forty-seven and went into a steep climb. "Swindal roared the big ship up to an unusually high cruising altitude of 41,000 feet where at 625 miles an hour, ground speed, the jet hurtled toward Andrews Air Force Base outside Washington," wrote Smith, whose reporting later earned him the Pulitzer Prize.

The flight east was fast and deathly quiet. Aides and secret service agents were leaden with shock. "I watched those Kennedy aides in total unfathomable grief, so deep and so penetrating beyond measure," Johnson aide Jack Valenti recalled. "It was totally unexpected. One minute they were in the shadow of the sun. The next, in darkness."

The new president and first lady comfort Mrs. Kennedy on board Air Force One. Judge Hughes is at left.

Some tried to comfort Mrs. Kennedy. She received them stoically, but several people who went to see her broke down themselves. An inevitable gulf developed between the Kennedy and Johnson contingents. Fehmer remembered that amid an awful hush, preparing an arrival statement was like "typing in the Pope's chapel."

The news media broadcast that the plane carrying the new and late presidents was in the air; they didn't know and couldn't say precisely where. Air bases along the way were on alert, but Air Force One flew high above the country alone, unescorted by fighter jets. By the time it reached the mid-south, the sun was going down.

The aircraft's sophisticated communications center was constantly in use. Army Major General Chester V. Clifton arranged for the arrival at Andrews and transporting the body to the Bethesda naval hospital, both in suburban Maryland. Another government plane carrying the secretary of state and an American delegation to a conference in Japan was turned around over the Pacific west of Hawaii. It, too, headed home for Washington.

President and Lady Bird Johnson called Rose Kennedy, the dead president's mother. "We feel like the heart has been cut out of us," Mrs. Johnson told her. The Johnsons also spoke with Nellie Connally, wife of John Connally, the Texas governor badly wounded in the assassination. "We are praying for you, darling, and I know that everything is going to be all right, isn't it?" the president said. "Give him a hug and a kiss for me."

"It was dark when Air Force One began to skim over the lights of the Washington area," Smith wrote, "lining up for a landing at Andrews Air Force Base."

The original plan was for an army helicopter from the White House executive flight detachment to ferry the president's body to the naval hospital. Knowing of Lyndon Johnson's history of heart trouble, a navy doctor also dispatched an ambulance to stand by. When Mrs. Kennedy decided that her husband's body should be driven to Bethesda, the navy ambulance was commandeered.

The floodlights at Andrews were doused at six o'clock to avoid blinding Swindal; "in the pale glow of a quarter moon," *Newsweek* reported, "the plane taxied like a gray ghost to the landing apron." The door opened and Robert Kennedy, the president's brother and attorney general, left a military truck and raced up the ramp. He brushed past Lyndon Johnson in search of Mrs. Kennedy.

General Clifton had radioed ahead for a forklift to help remove the bronze casket. Andrews instead sent out a boxy catering truck, a logical but unsuitable choice. The vehicle—"glistening yellow on the outside, dazzling white on the inside, framed with lights of white and red," author Theodore White wrote—maneuvered up beside Air Force One flanked by one of Bird's teams. The enclosed cargo lift rose to the aircraft's rear door.

Unloading the casket at Andrews Air Force Base.

Lieutenant Bird entered the plane with body bearers he had picked to carry the president's casket from the plane to the tarmac. He was dismayed to find that the casket wasn't covered with a flag and was being "poorly handled." Bird saluted Brigadier General Godfrey McHugh, the air force aide. Devastated by the assassination, McHugh had exclaimed while on the ground in Dallas, "I have only one president, and he's lying back in that cabin." He had stood with the casket as an honor guard on the flight back to Andrews.

McHugh brusquely ordered Bird to clear the area—the aides, advisors and agents would carry the casket off the plane. Overcome by "maudlin Irish sentiment," the late president's political advisor and longtime friend Kenneth O'Donnell had made the decision only as they were landing. Although prevented from doing their duty, Bird's body bearers on the truck understood the gesture and quickly obeyed the lieutenant's order to give way to the president's men. "They were in earnest and they were hurting," Marine Private First Class Jerry J. Diamond recalled of the aides long afterward.

Still distraught, McHugh shoved Sergeant Felder aside. But the general and the Irish contingent weren't as fit or adept as Bird's men. They had damaged the casket at Love Field in wrestling it from the hearse and up the ramp. Their task was equally awkward here. McHugh's volunteers strained to carry the unwieldy casket into the lift, aided by Bird and two men he had kept behind.

Mrs. Kennedy and her brother-in-law stepped into the enclosed compartment of the catering truck after them. The television cameras found her there, clutching Robert Kennedy's hand. One of her later biographers, a schoolgirl in 1963, remembered the gasp in the family living room at the sight of her blood-spattered skirt and stockings. To *New York Times* photographer Tames, Mrs. Kennedy symbolized all women who had lost a husband or son in battle.

The lift slowly descended but stopped at chest height, the lowest it could go. Several of the civilians jumped down to the tarmac, leaving the casket momentarily on the floor. When they struggled to pick it up again and wobbled under the burden, Sam Bird responded as only an angry, decisive lieutenant would ever dare. He ignored the general's wishes and sent help anyway.

His body bearers raced in to displace or support whomever

they could. "There was more hauling as military men and civilians sought to lend a hand," reported the *New York Times*, "as though by this last act they could help the president." Staff Sergeant Gaudreau found a grip and helped slide the casket into the ambulance, Lance Corporal Cheek behind him amid the agents.

Lieutenant Bird, a lone symbol of efficiency and ceremony amid the confusion, saluted from atop the truck.

Once the casket was loaded, Captain Tazewell Shepard, the late president's naval aide, lifted Mrs. Kennedy down to the tarmac. "I'll never forget the anguish on her face," he said years later. Unwilling to leave her husband's body to ride to the hospital in a limousine, she walked alone to the gray ambulance and tried a rear passenger door, which was locked.

"She stood there, so slim, so very straight, so all alone, and someone opened the door from within," reported the *Washington Daily News*.

When she was seated inside and the curtains drawn, the ambulance moved off across the tarmac, escorted by secret service cars and police motorcycles. The new president stood almost unnoticed near the doorway of Air Force One. Only after the procession had left did he emerge to address the nation.

Sam Bird and his commanding general were no longer there to hear him.

BETHESDA

With the president's body headed to Bethesda, General Wehle hustled onto a nearby helicopter with Lipsey, Bird and his joint-service casket team. The rest of the Old Guard troops who had flown over from Fort Myer hopped aboard a second chopper.

Each aircraft was an H-21 Shawnee, an army cargo transport with two large rotors. Soldiers called these machines Flying Bananas. Wehle's was fitted with cushioned seats for transporting dignitaries and every seat was taken. The craft lifted off into the night amid its rotor wash and noise.

General Wehle was a West Pointer, Class of 1930. He had brought Lipsey north with him to Washington from his previous command at Fort Polk, Louisiana. The aide admired the general, but Lipsey didn't want to be riding in this helicopter or thinking about the air traffic crowding the skies over the capital.

"We had two lieutenants flying that thing who were younger than I was and I was young," Lipsey recalled. "I was scared to death."

The H-21 reached Bethesda within minutes and began

its descent toward the hospital. The helipad there was new, built two years before and never used. Word had spread that the president's body was expected and many people assumed the helicopter was bringing it. Lipsey was shocked to see a sea of faces surrounding the helipad. He watched police below herd the civilians away and feared that if anything went wrong "we'd cut off four thousand people's heads." The young pilot set the Shawnee down expertly.

"I know he had been scared to death, too," Lipsey said later. "There was no room or margin for error when he set that helicopter down." Although he flew frequently in military and civilian life afterwards, Lipsey for years was haunted by visions of "landing that helicopter in all those people."

Back at Andrews Air Force Base, Lyndon Johnson was making his brief remarks amid the lights and the noise. The few paces to the bank of microphones, *Time* ventured, "must have seemed the loneliest, longest walk of his life."

"This is a sad time for all people," the new president said. "We have suffered a loss that cannot be weighed. For me it is a deep personal tragedy. I know the world shares the sorrow that Mrs. Kennedy and her family bear. I will do my best. That is all I can do. I ask for your help—and God's."

After pausing to speak with old colleagues from the congress, the Texan boarded Army One, a handsome green-and-white army VH-3A Sea King helicopter. The craft lifted off for the seven-minute flight to the White House.

Merriman Smith got onto another helicopter from the executive fleet. Advisor Theodore Sorensen was also on board, looking ashen and lost. Author of much of the late president's soaring rhetoric, Sorensen had gone to the air base to meet the body. He now sat weeping during the short flight back; he said bitterly to a Johnson aide, "I hate that goddamned state of Texas of yours." As the helicopter approached the White House, Smith found it incredible that only few hours earlier "John Fitzgerald Kennedy had been a vibrant, smiling, waving and active man."

President Johnson's secretary Marie Fehmer also found the first hour in Washington distressing. Lost in a kaleidoscope of lights, noises and unfamiliar people, she was unable to say later whether she had flown to the White House on the president's helicopter or on another. She landed on the south lawn and quickly got separated from everyone she knew.

Fehmer worked in the vice president's office next door in the executive office building and wasn't familiar with the White House. In a sort of waking nightmare, worried that she might accidentally break something or trip the hot line to the Kremlin, she wandered alone through the silent mansion. She passed through a diplomatic reception area, the west basement and the cabinet room, but saw no one who could help her. "Maybe I did see people and just didn't ask," she said later.

The secretary eventually found her way back outside and identified herself to a White House driver. She asked him to take her home. Years later, Fehmer wondered aloud during an interview why the secret service had "let me wander all over that building."

Bethesda was even more disorganized than the mansion. The hospital staff first expected the president's body to arrive by helicopter and formed a cordon of sailors from the helipad to the rear morgue entrance. When the ambulance was on the way, word was put out that it would arrive at the emergency entrance to mislead the press. Lipsey and others later recalled that a decoy ambulance was also sent "because we knew there was a mob waiting." A somber

crowd did surround the facility, but the "second ambulance" may have been the result of confusion and miscom-
munication. Bird made no mention of it in his later report.

The gray ambulance with the president's body arrived
from Andrews at six fifty-three. Bird's plan to place an army
cordon at the front entrance was thwarted by the "tremen-
dous crowd," but sailors lining the drive delivered a hand
salute as the ambulance passed. Navy officers then escorted
Mrs. Kennedy and the attorney general to a suite on the
seventeenth floor of the hospital tower. To the *Washington
Evening Star*, she seemed to wear "the slight, crushed smile
of the bereaved."

Lieutenant Bird's casket team was waiting tensely in a
guard truck when the ambulance arrived. Mrs. Kennedy
wanted the autopsy and embalming performed here
at Bethesda rather than at the funeral home. Navy duty
officers riding with the casket team had expected the ambulance to follow their truck to the morgue, located at a
rear entrance. But with masses of people obstructing movement and vision, the plan went awry.

"Retracing our path, we found the ambulance still at the
front of the hospital amid many onlookers," a navy phar-
macologist wrote later. "In our haste we had left without
confirming that the ambulance was behind us. On the
second try we did it right."

"For at least 12 minutes after Mrs. Kennedy entered the
hospital," the *Star* reported, "the ambulance remained in
the driveway. Many spectators could see the simple casket
within."

The ambulance eventually reached the rear entrance and
Bird formed up his team to carry the casket to the morgue.
Still unwilling to leave the president's body, McHugh
ordered Yeoman Barnum aside and took the coastie's place
at the casket. The burden was no lighter than at Andrews

and McHugh was fifty-two years old. The general finally gave up and motioned Barnum back. The team continued through the corridors to the navy morgue.

Doctors laid the president's body on a table. He was the first dead man Lipsey had ever seen. It was "a pretty traumatic experience," he recalled, but the general had ordered him to remain for the autopsy and Lipsey obeyed. No one challenged his or Bird's presence in the room. Years later, congressional investigators would question Lipsey closely about what he witnessed this night, the first time he ever spoke of it.

The autopsy continued for hours as Lipsey fought his queasiness and tried to ignore the smell of formaldehyde. Neither lieutenant had eaten since morning and Bird sent a man out for food. "We sat in there watching part of the autopsy eating hamburgers," Lipsey remembered.

Along with a detachment of marines, Bird's six body bearers were posted as guards in the corridors and at the two doors into the autopsy room. Felder was in charge of his six-man team. The sergeant had first glimpsed the president on a torrid summer day in 1962, during a review in which several sailors had passed out in the sun. Tradition dictated leaving them there, but the commander-in-chief had sent officers scrambling with a barked order, "Get these men out of the heat."

Felder had occasionally served as a presidential orderly after that, had answered the time-honored questions about his hometown and the quality of the chow. He had found in the president "my hero and political inspiration" and had wept upon hearing of his death. Determined to guard their commander-in-chief's privacy, the sergeant and the other body bearers protected the morgue with the grimness of linebackers.

The team ejected an imposter doctor. Felder and Specialist

Mayfield bodily tossed two photographers out a door. They took satisfaction later in knowing that the best photo the press got was of an empty stretcher that had nothing to do with the president.

In the hospital's tower suite, Mrs. Kennedy's thoughts turned to the funeral. She had helped prepare a White House guidebook for tourists and remembered an illustration of Abraham Lincoln's body lying on a catafalque in the East Room. When Robert Kennedy suggested that they consider arrangements for the president, she replied, "It's in the guidebook."

At the White House, Shriver soon learned of the vague remark. "Sarge" had been managing the crisis in the mansion since late afternoon, issuing orders to military personnel and civilians alike. Calls went out now to the Library of Congress.

No request made by Mrs. Kennedy or in her name during these days had any authority in law. Many actually came from Shriver, the attorney general, or aides. Yet all were honored without hesitation. No one in MDW or official Washington denied Mrs. Kennedy anything she requested or was said to want. It was nearing midnight when a pair of researchers met at the entrance to the great library opposite the Capitol.

Dr. David C. Mearns was head of the library's manuscript division and editor of the Lincoln papers. Professor James I. Robertson, Jr. was the executive director of the civil war centennial commission. The White House could hardly have found two more prominent or knowledgeable scholars to delve into the Lincoln funeral.

Working alone, Mearns and Robertson discovered that after normal library hours a timer controlled the lighting. The pair "wandered through the bowels of that cavernous building armed only with flashlights," Robertson recalled, pulling down yellowing magazine and newspaper accounts from the previous century. Washington poet Joe Osterhaus wondered forty years later:

> *Those flashlights, improvising to the beat of those first*
> *few hours:*
> *how visible were their incisions from the empty street?*
> *What made that random lightstorm beautiful?*

The articles the pair uncovered became the guide for redecorating the East Room, the largest in the mansion. An odd, egalitarian group then began hanging yards of black crepe from the chandeliers, mantels and doorways. Led by Kennedy family friend William Walton—"the New Frontier's artist-without-portfolio," historian William Manchester called him later—they also hastily arranged flowers and candlesticks. The volunteers included advisors, aides, military officers, historians, undertakers, domestic staff, an upholsterer, the mansion's dog handler, ceremonies chief Miller and Shriver.

The original Lincoln catafalque was needed at the Capitol, but a replica had been built for the interment of the unknown soldiers from World War II and Korea in 1958. General Wehle ordered its retrieval from storage at Arlington National Cemetery. A detail from Fort Myer delivered the pieces and assembled the catafalque in the East Room. The Walton team adapted other Lincoln details to modern tastes and circumstances. As a final touch, a White House driver fetched a Benedictine cross from Shriver's bedroom.

General Wehle had served in both the Pacific and European theaters during World War II and attended the war college during Korea. He had briefly served as the army's chief of field artillery. Now after a third of a century as a commissioned officer, he was fifty-seven years old and nearing the end of his career.

Busy making calls, Wehle was in and out of the Bethesda morgue all night. He returned as the autopsy ended and asked Lipsey if he wanted a break. The aide left for ten or fifteen minutes and found a telephone. In the middle of the night, the shaken young lieutenant called his parents long distance and woke them.

"Guess where I am or what I just did?" he said. "I just watched Kennedy's autopsy."

The elder Lipseys replied that they had seen him on television at Andrews. Lipsey told them he would also take part in the funeral and to keep watching. "That was the sum total of my reaction to my parents," he said later. "I didn't discuss anything about anything."

Lipsey sat with Bird while morticians from Gawler's performed their tasks. The general's driver went to the White House to pick up fresh clothing for the body. A valet came back with several suits; aides chose the president's favorite, one he had called his "tv suit." Aides also went to Gawler's to select a casket to replace the one marred *en route* from Dallas.

"I always thought my funeral would be great because President Kennedy would come to it," assistant David Powers said sadly. "And now here I am, helping to pick out his casket." In 1966, the original Dallas casket would be quietly discarded at sea.

At the naval hospital, Lipsey helped the morticians dress the body. After all they had seen in the past hours, the initials JFK monogrammed on the sleeve of a crisp white shirt somehow struck Bird hard. It was four a.m. when the morticians finished.

Gawler's supplied Bird's team with a standard veterans administration American flag, five and a half feet by nine feet. The men draped it over the new mahogany casket, where it would remain through all the transport and ceremonies until reaching the graveside. The lieutenant noticed a name stamped on the white hem: Valley Forge Flag Company. Days later, he wrote to the manufacturers in Pennsylvania to tell them about their flag.

Word was passed upstairs in the hospital and shortly before four a.m. Mrs. Kennedy descended from the tower. Again she got into the ambulance with the casket. "Still had on the pink suit—she hadn't changed clothes," Lipsey remembered later. A police car led the small caravan away from the hospital at five minutes before the hour. General Wehle's staff car came next, then the ambulance and a family car or two. Military vehicles blocked the roads to stop anyone following.

Across town, White House staffers, assistants and reporters stood a vigil at the mansion, awaiting the president's return. Among them was a longtime telephone operator who had helped answer hundreds of calls until going off duty at two in the morning.

"I just had to stay to see him home," she said. "It's my way of paying respects."

Balls were not so much being dropped by MDW and the White House as not being put into play. Little in ceremonies chief Miller's manual covered the events of the past several hours. With the president's body now expected at the mansion shortly before dawn, Shriver was appalled to learn that no one had arranged for an honor guard to escort the ambulance inside the grounds. Captain Shepard made an urgent call to the Marine Barracks.

The barracks stood at Eighth and I streets in southeast Washington. President Thomas Jefferson had personally chosen the site in 1801, near the navy yard and "within easy marching distance of the Capitol." Now home of the commandant, the Marine Band and other tenants, it was the oldest post in the corps.

The late president had inspected the "Eighth and Eye" marines at their barracks one memorable night in July 1962. Since the Marine Band was the only unit he commanded directly, he had said, together they would "hold the White House against all odds, at least for some time to come." The quip was sadly inaccurate and now the barracks was preparing for his funeral.

Officers were puzzled that they hadn't already received orders from the White House to send an honor guard. Being good marines, they had put a team on standby. An officer recalled later that the silent drill platoon, a ceremonial unit, had turned in that night with "shoes and brass shined, dress blues hanging nearby and M-1 rifles drawn."

The young marines leapt from their racks when the phone rang finally around three-thirty. Lieutenant Colonel Miller sent a bus and armed forces police to escort them. They squared away their uniforms and equipment on the bus during the dash across Washington and arrived at the White House in just eighteen minutes.

In the predawn darkness, the dozen marines quickly formed two ranks under First Lieutenant William Lee. He marched them down the curved drive, stopped near the gate and spoke to the platoon there. Aides watched from the mansion as the marines bowed their heads.

Round black flare pots, borrowed from the district's highway department, illuminated the drive. The ambulance arrived at the northwest gate at four twenty-seven and the marines escorted it to the North Portico. As they marched slowly at port arms, said the Associated Press, "all that could be heard was the sound of their shoes sliding on the macadam." The platoon's solemn perfection was expected, but arriving in time to escort the president home became barracks legend.

The body bearers, too, knew the meaning of *Semper fidelis*. Their duty was difficult. Unlike British military funerals, in which the casket was borne on the shoulders, in the United States it was carried waist-high and from the side. Old Guard teams at Fort Myer trained with weighted caskets to lessen the strain on their arms, shoulders and backs. But the emotional challenges were equally hard.

The joint-service team of six body bearers assembled by Lieutenant Bird enters the White House.

Any casket team wanted perfection for a family, whether it was a private's or the president's. Not everyone can maintain the composure necessary to performing amid public grief. "This kind of duty," Sergeant Felder later wrote, "tends to make a man cold, callous and emotionless." The pressure on a team carrying a president's casket before the eyes of the nation and much of the world was unimaginable, yet each body bearer did his best to ignore it.

Several of the men on the joint-service team Bird had assembled at Andrews had worked together before. This was an advantage, but the distance from the portico, through the lobby and down a long hallway to the East Wing was more than the few usual paces from caisson to gravesite. Felder suddenly realized that the Gawler's casket was the heaviest he had ever handled, much heavier than standard military caskets. The six enlisted men struggled with the weight, perhaps as much as twelve hundred pounds.

As the officer commanding the team, Lieutenant Bird walked behind the casket but did not touch it. Seeing his men lurch as they entered the White House, he did something extraordinary. Violating Old Guard protocol, he stepped forward to grasp the casket himself, at the head where the weight was greatest.

"Good god, don't let go!" a body bearer implored in a whisper.

Bird's hands were still beneath the president's casket as his team entered the East Room. He likely considered the moment an aberration, an emergency caused by stress and weight and exhaustion. But several times during the next two and a half days, Bird again helped his team by supporting the casket. The body bearers never forgot it.

Sam Bird, Felder remembered, was "a soldier's soldier."

SATURDAY

NOVEMBER 23

WASHINGTON

With daylight and perhaps an hour or two of fitful sleep for a few, Washington began regaining its balance. Plans changed and evolved over the weekend, sometimes quickly, but nothing equaled the disarray of Friday. Already, it was time to move ahead despite the gloom.

Saturday's skies matched the public mood. Friday had been "a hazy Indian summer day . . . possibly a last brush with nature before bad weather sets in," a Scripps-Howard reporter wrote. Overnight a cold front had rushed in behind Air Force One; now, said *The Washington Post*, "a shroud of rain fell over Washington."

A private memorial service was set for ten-thirty in the East Room. Invitations went out by phone and telegrams to officials and diplomats to pay their respects after the family. A schedule was announced. The hours between eleven o'clock and two were reserved for the executive branch, presidential appointees and White House staff. Two to two-thirty saw the justices of the supreme court. From two-thirty until five, senators, members of congress, and state and territorial governors paid their respects. The chiefs of the diplomatic missions followed until seven p.m.

The White House entrances were draped in black and troops lined the corridor to the East Room. As at any other home visited by tragedy, cars, taxis and limousines filled the drive; mourners received tickets to retrieve their vehicles afterward. "Nation's Great File Past Kennedy Bier," said a headline in *The Washington Post*. The *Star* also noted that "humbler citizens kept their own vigil outside in the rain," a crowd of several hundred standing silently along Pennsylvania Avenue and in Lafayette Park.

All day, the important and the powerful passed through the East Room. "So much history is taking place in so short a time," said NBC's Frank McGee. Dwight Eisenhower arrived from Gettysburg and in a display of bipartisanship met briefly with the new president. Harry Truman came from Independence and stayed across the street at Blair House. Lawmakers, diplomats and jurists came and went. The death watch changed every thirty minutes. A twelve-year-old who accompanied his father thought the casket seemed "much too small to hold a President."

Allies and enemies alike filed through the mansion. New York Governor Nelson Rockefeller attended, as did a segregationist counterpart, Governor George Wallace of Alabama. U.S. Senator Clair Engle of California, dying of a brain tumor, arrived in a wheelchair. Sergeant Felder noticed Senator Hubert H. Humphrey, the "happy warrior" from Minnesota, who was crying. For all his experience during perhaps a thousand military funerals, the sergeant nearly broke down himself.

"As the gloomy afternoon wore on, the White House took on a strangely desolate appearance," the *Star* said, "with shades drawn and flag at half-mast." Throughout the day, the enormous East Room remained dim and quiet, "an utter, complete quiet that seemed to grip—well, the whole country, I suppose," Mrs. Johnson wrote.

The death watch stands by the casket in the East Room on Saturday, November 23.

At Robert Kennedy's request, soldiers from the army's special forces—the "green berets"—were integrated into the death watch. The attorney general understood his brother's interest in the unconventional troops. The president had overruled the army to authorize their distinctive headgear, which he had called "a symbol of excellence, a badge of courage, a mark of distinction in the fight for freedom."

Brigadier General William P. Yarborough was the special forces' commander. Slightly built, dapper and tough, he had been on a flight from New York to his headquarters at Fort Bragg, North Carolina, when he learned of the shooting. By the time Yarborough landed, the president was dead and the armed forces were on a heightened state of alert. The news erased the green berets' swagger. "These boys regard the president as their godfather," an officer said later.

General Yarborough received telephoned orders on Saturday to rush a contingent of green beret soldiers to Washington. Late that afternoon, an air force C-130 Hercules aircraft lifted off and headed north from Fort Bragg. On board were Colonel William Grieves, Command Sergeant Major Francis J. Ruddy and forty-two other enlisted men and two officers representing the Fifth, Sixth and Seventh Special Forces Groups.

The Old Guard quickly established a "death-watch school" in the White House basement to teach the green berets and other troops how to handle the unfamiliar duty. Captain Groves, commander of the honor guard company, also set up a command post in the mansion's theater.

The oval shoulder patch worn by army troops assigned to the Military District of Washington resembled a park service logo: against a blue sky, a red sword lay across the white Washington Monument, with a rounded green hill at the bottom. Headquarters later relocated entirely to Fort McNair, but now also occupied quarters on Second Street SW.

Despite gaps and inadequacies, Colonel Miller's manual, *State, Official and Special Military Funeral Policies and Plans*, provided MDW with a few firm guideposts for the coming days. Military and civilian crews prepared the Capitol for the president's body to lie in state at the rotunda on Sunday. Workers from the architect of the capitol's office dusted the huge oil paintings and marble statuary, silently watched by a statue of President James Garfield, assassinated eighty-two years earlier.

Others brought the Lincoln catafalque up from beneath the Capitol, where it was stored in an unused crypt originally intended for George Washington. The bier had borne the casket of the Great Emancipator nearly a century before and various presidents and dignitaries since, including Franklin Roosevelt in 1945. A civilian fitter from the quartermaster maintenance shop at Fort Myer, Mary Scott of southeast Washington, mended small tears in the catafalque's black velvet and broadcloth.

Across the river at Fort Meyer, troops of the Old Guard drilled in the rain. By unspoken agreement, all stubbornly refused to wear raincoats over their olive-drab fatigues as they rehearsed their movements and march steps.

Unlike regular line units, the regiment also issued enlisted men formal uniforms called dress blues, which they wore routinely and faultlessly. An exasperated sergeant in Nicholas Proffitt's novel *Gardens of Stone* later called the Third Infantry the "silliest goddamn outfit in the United States Army . . . nothing but a bunch of toy soldiers." But it was a mistake actually to think of them that way.

All of the troops were qualified infantrymen and the unit, formed in 1784, was the oldest in the army. General Winfield Scott had bestowed the nickname "the Old Guard" in 1847 after bloody campaigning in the Mexican war. They were also identifiable in their blues by a unique, tan-and-black "buff strap" worn on the left shoulder, a relic of the knapsacks they had once carried in the field. In formation, the men marched with fixed bayonets gleaming, whereas other units' bayonets were always sheathed.

The Old Guard at Fort Myer wasn't a full-sized regiment but a smaller, reinforced battalion or "battle group"— officially, First Battalion (reinforced), Third Infantry. In addition to their ceremonial duties, its companies regularly slipped into the woods and hills of Virginia for field exercises. The troops called themselves the "Third Herd."

If accustomed to the public eye, members of the Old Guard were no less wisecracking, irreverent or cynical than any young soldiers; they simply concealed that fact behind a perfectly tailored and spit-shined facade. Many did possess, however, an old-fashioned sense of honor. The mission they drilled for now would be remembered more than any other in the Old Guard's long history.

Military musicians were also preparing. Each of the five armed services had at least one band. The marines possessed the senior group, established by an act of congress in 1798. The Marine Band had performed at the White House before its construction was finished, playing for John Adams on New Year's Day in 1801. Marine bandsmen had accompanied Lincoln to Gettysburg. John Philip Sousa himself had once been its director.

Like the Old Guard, the Marine Band carried a proud nickname, "The President's Own." Stretching back to President Jefferson, the title had proved especially apt during the past three years. The late president had enjoyed the band and summoned it often to the mansion. Mrs. Kennedy had influenced what and how the scarlet-coated musicians had performed, giving the band a unique social role at the White House.

Nonplussed at receiving civilian instructions that contradicted his military orders, a young marine captain had once pleaded with Letitia Baldrige, the first lady's social secretary, to "think of the predicament. You're a girl—and hell, I mean, excuse me, ma'am, the general is my commanding officer here."

The U.S. Army Band was a century and a quarter younger than its marine counterpart. Known as "Pershing's Own," it was formed by order of General John J. "Black Jack" Pershing in 1922 to emulate the bands he had heard in Europe during World War I. The band performed overseas in the second world war, earning a battle streamer during the Rhineland campaign. In the fifties, singers Eddie Fisher and Steve Lawrence performed with the band and Charles Osgood had announced for the chorus.

As the senior service, the army coordinated all the military bands for the funeral. The job went to Captain Gilbert H. Mitchell, the Army Band's executive officer and associate conductor. "It was a sad time," he recalled many years later. "It was a very exciting time. You were involved twenty-four hours a day."

The captain informed General Wehle that all of the drums used in the funeral must be shrouded in black. But the bands used drums of various sizes, and nobody had black drapes or shrouds ready. Mitchell obtained the dimensions for all the drums and called in his "very capable" supply sergeant. The clothing and equipment shop at Fort Myer worked up the shrouds overnight.

"I used to do slip covers and draperies, to cover furniture," seamstress Viola Williams Canady recalled, so creating shrouds for drums wasn't difficult. After her team finished at four o'clock in the morning, she returned on Sunday to help prepare the black bunting and tassels for the artillery caisson that would carry the casket.

The Old Guard's Fife and Drum Corps was also busy. Formed just three years earlier, the small ceremonial band played colonial music and wore period uniforms complete with wigs and tricorn hats. Its drums were custom-made by a craftsman in Baltimore whose great-grandfather had made drums for the army in the civil war. The unit had rushed out to Andrews Air Force Base on Friday evening along with many others, but had not performed.

Now, as in the larger bands, the corps' drummers not only draped but also muffled their instruments. Tension was maintained on the drumheads with ropes. To muffle his drum, a soldier loosened the tension and turned off the wires, or snares, that caused its distinctive rattle. But as with so much else, what role the drummers and fifers would perform in the funeral wasn't yet clear.

The Air Force Pipe Band was back at Bolling, having landed from New Orleans about one a.m. It was another young band, formed just five years earlier. The pipers also had been something of a favorite of the commander-in-chief's and the regard was mutual. Airman Sandy Jones had recently composed a special pipe tune for him: *President Kennedy's Welcome to Sean Lemass*. The president and the visiting Irish prime minister for whom it was titled had both autographed the sheet music. The bandsmen now wanted and expected to participate in the funeral. They would do so, but these kilted American airmen wouldn't be the only pipers playing.

The bagpipers of the British Army's famed Black Watch (Royal Highland Regiment) had performed on the South Lawn of the White House for seventeen hundred children just ten days earlier. "On Potomac's Bonnie Banks," the *New York Times* had quipped in a caption beneath its front-page photo. "Highland Fling Is Flung at Home of Clan Kennedy," said *The Washington Post*.

The event had marked the first lady's first public appearance since the death in August of her newborn son, Patrick. Although she had gone abroad to recover, photos taken that day showed her looking pensive beside her husband. Caroline and John Junior enjoyed the colorful uniforms and skirling music, however, and watched with their parents from the mansion's balcony. Caroline had curtsied to Major W. M. Wingate Gray, the detachment's commander, imposing in his kilt, white stockings and tall, bearskin Busby, then climbed back into her father's lap for the performance. John fingered the major's medals and briefly sat in his lap.

The Black Watch's Latin motto was *Nemo me impune*

lacessi, which they translated as "Nobody wounds us with impunity." The president had added, "I think that is a very good motto for some of the rest of us." He took to the Black Watch pipers as readily as his children. "I don't know when I have seen the President enjoy himself more," the first lady wrote to the major afterward. She later kept a photo of the occasion in a silver frame.

Mrs. Kennedy thought of the Black Watch on the flight home from Dallas and said they must be at the funeral. Now on Saturday Letitia Baldrige called Knoxville, the current stop on the pipers' American tour. Would a portion of the hundred-twenty-man detachment return to Washington?

The invitation was unprecedented—almost unthinkable in other circumstances—and the chain of command so convoluted that Queen Elizabeth personally had to approve her army's participation. Buckingham Palace quickly agreed. The Black Watch replied that it was sending nine pipers to Washington and the musicians offered to pay their own airfares. They were soon on their way back east from Tennessee.

The Black Watch wouldn't be the sole foreign contingent. On Air Force One, Mrs. Kennedy also spoke of the president's June trip to Ireland and how he was moved by a silent drill performed at Arbour Hill in Dublin by Irish army cadets. They, too, must be part of the funeral. General Clifton called the Irish ambassador. The Military College at Curragh swiftly agreed to send an officer and thirty members of the Thirty-seventh Cadet Class. Irish International Air said it would fly them over on the same plane bringing President de Valera. The Old Guard cleared quarters for the teenaged cadets in Company B's barracks at Fort Myer.

Accepting Scottish and Irish participation in the state funeral of a president couldn't have been easy for the Pentagon, but not a murmur was heard publicly. "The American forces are no less jealous of their prerogatives than others," noted *The Times* of London, but were "generous to the last" in welcoming the cadets and the Black Watch pipers, the latter "symbolizing the special relationship between Britain and the United States."

Saturday was also the day for determining a burial site. The assumption was that the president's body would be taken home to Massachusetts. There was ample sentiment for this among the Kennedy family and aides. The *Boston Globe* and others thought interment might be in the family plot at Holyhood Cemetery in Brookline outside Boston. A crypt and monument on the Boston Commons was another possibility. A navy destroyer was standing by to ferry the casket north and a funeral train was also discussed.

Robert McNamara, the secretary of defense, believed to the contrary that the president should be buried on federal land at Arlington. He decided to visit the cemetery himself on Saturday morning. By the time McNamara arrived, MDW ceremonies chief Paul Miller and John C. Metzler, the cemetery's superintendent, had settled on three likely burial plots. McNamara rejected locations near Dewey Circle and the USS *Maine* monument, preferring a site on the slope below Arlington House, the stately old Custis-Lee mansion.

Before the civil war, this had been the home of Virginian Robert E. Lee and his wife, Mary Custis. Turning down command of the Union army, Lee went south to fight for the Confederacy, never to return. The government seized the property in the war and Quartermaster General Montgomery C. Meigs transformed it into a military cemetery.

Among the Union soldiers buried there was Meigs' son, killed in the Shenandoah Valley. In the century since, Arlington had become hallowed ground, the national burial ground for heroes, ordinary GIs and spouses. Acre after rolling acre, simple headstones and monuments dotted the hills like stone flowers, more than one hundred twenty thousand now.

McNamara visited the cemetery three more times on Saturday in the pouring rain. He was accompanied at various hours by military officers, family members and advisors. Robert Kennedy, his sisters Pat and Jean, and Bill Walton joined him on the second trip. Mrs. Kennedy went on the third, at about two o'clock. She had a fondness for the spot; the mansion was the first place daughter Caroline had learned to recognize on coming to Washington.

Mrs. Kennedy approved. So did artist Walton, who pointed to a precise spot on the grass and said, "This is perfect." Metzler drove a wooden stake to mark the location.

On his fourth visit late in the day, McNamara met Paul Fuqua, a college student who worked as a park service tour guide at Arlington House and whose father worked for the defense department. The young man told McNamara about an impromptu visit the president had made to the mansion the previous spring.

"The president didn't know the story of how the Memorial Bridge links Abraham Lincoln and Robert E. Lee, pulling the two sides of the Civil War together," Fuqua recalled long afterward. The two had chatted about that. Then the president said that the view of Washington across the Potomac was so beautiful that "I could stay up here forever." Fuqua repeated the remark to McNamara. It seemed to confirm that the slope at Arlington was the right site for the burial.

"Only the nine-inch wooden stake marked the late President's gravesite last night," wrote a reporter for *The Washington Post* who had located McNamara's party in the rain and failing light. His article on Sunday pinpointed the location and provided a small map. It added that five more stakes "will be driven into the ground when dawn brings light for the surveyors." These surveyors later determined that the site was almost perfectly aligned with the mansion and the Lincoln Memorial across the river.

By Saturday evening, MDW had a direct liaison with Mrs. Kennedy and the attorney general and "their wishes were ascertained and incorporated into existing plans," army historians Mossman and Stark wrote. With this, "arrangements for the remaining funeral ceremonies assumed definite shape."

Any inter-service rivalries or jealousies within MDW or the Pentagon were put aside. Ceremonies chief Miller later reported that the "total cooperation of all branches of the Armed Forces was superb."

SUNDAY

NOVEMBER 24

CAPITOL

The rain swept out of the capital and gave way to brilliant sunshine. It was forty-six degrees by noon Sunday, what some people called Kennedy weather. The president's casket was scheduled to be escorted up Pennsylvania Avenue to the Capitol at one o'clock.

"Nice day for a procession," said a woman in Lafayette Park.

"He'd have loved it," agreed a motorcycle cop.

General Wehle, the MDW commander, had approved Sergeant Felder's suggestion to add two men to the six-man casket team originally assembled Friday night at Andrews Air Force Base. The additions were marine Jerry Diamond and navy Seaman Apprentice Larry B. Smith, both experienced body bearers. The team, now eight strong, also had a wheeled church truck to use inside the White House, away from the view of television cameras.

Troops lined the drive outside the mansion and the nearly two miles up Pennsylvania and Constitution avenues to the Capitol. The army, navy, marines and air force each assigned two hundred forty officers and men to the duty.

The navy also posted roving first-aid crews along the way. The cortege, or ceremonial escort, comprised two hundred seventeen men, who now stood at attention on the great semicircular drive. Planning had been so quick and improvised that the Old Guard captain in charge at the White House had the details of events jotted on the back of an envelope in his pocket.

Ten limousines waited to take the Kennedy family, President Johnson, the new first lady, friends, staff and secret service agents up to the Capitol. At eight minutes after one, after a final few moments of privacy for the family in the East Room, the body bearers wheeled the president's flag-draped casket through a joint-services honor cordon to the North Portico. They emerged into the sunlight carrying the casket and strapped it onto a black Third Infantry caisson, built in 1918 for the army field artillery during the Great War.

The entire cortege left the White House through an archway of fifty-four state and territorial flags held by navy bandsmen. Each flag rose in turn as the caisson approached, and "fluttered strongly, too splendidly gay," said *The Washington Post*. A contingent of 60 metropolitan police led the way on foot, followed by General Wehle and two army officers at the head of the troops. With his stocky build, snowy hair and sharply creased uniform, Wehle could have been mistaken for a gruff police captain himself.

To grant the family's request that muffled drums alone accompany the cortege up Pennsylvania Avenue, the services had assembled a special joint detail that army band Captain Mitchell called a "corps of drums." Initial plans called for four snare drummers from each of the five services. But the Navy Band was scheduled to perform upon the procession's arrival at the Capitol; it could spare only two men, so the Army Band sent six. The corps also included one army and one marine bass drummer, flanked by two additional snare drummers from the air force.

The musicians marched in six rows of four, each man in the uniform of his service; the marines were conspicuous in the second row for their scarlet coats. A navy drum major led the corps, which was commanded from the side by a navy lieutenant carrying a white baton. The procession had no other musicians, only the two-dozen drummers, whose ceaseless beat would leave them exhausted.

General Wehle had confided to Captain Mitchell at his command center Saturday night that he had never marched to drumbeats alone. Admiring his determination to leave no detail unrehearsed, Mitchell had linked arms with him and recited the drum cadence aloud. "For about ten minutes, we marched up and down those long halls," he recalled.

Marching behind the drums was a navy company of ninety-three officers and enlisted men, a nod to the late president's naval service during the war. General Maxwell Taylor led the joint chiefs of staff behind the sailors. Following the chiefs were the president's military aides, a joint-service color detail and three Washington clergymen.

Next came the rumbling caisson. The Old Guard stables had twenty-nine horses, both blacks and grays. Today, the team was six handsome matched grays, bought in Texas three years earlier by the Army Remount Service's last purchasing agent. All were saddled, but only the animals on the left had riders. A soldier on a seventh gray led the caisson. Rather than use heavy transport, the Old Guard had simply hitched up the team and driven the caisson down across the bridge and into downtown from Fort Myer.

Twenty-four enlisted servicemen flanked the caisson. A pair of Old Guard soldiers on each side led the escort. Two men from each of the five armed services marched on each side, arranged in order of the seniority of their services: army, marines, navy, air force, coast guard. The green uniforms and berets of the special forces stood out amid the shades of blue worn by the other troops.

Directly behind the caisson marched Seaman Apprentice Edward W. Nemuth, carrying the presidential flag on a tall standard. The nineteen-year-old from Livingstone, New Jersey, had served in the ceremonial guard at Anacostia Naval Station for just seven months. Assigned to carry the flag the night before, he hadn't had an opportunity to drill with the casket team. Behind Nemuth came Lieutenant Bird and his eight body bearers, then the riderless horse that signified a fallen leader.

In a military funeral, the horse is "caparisoned"— ceremonially equipped or covered. The tradition went as far back as Genghis Khan and Tamerlane. A black animal carried a saddle, bridle and blanket; a horse of any other color also carried a cape and hood. Riding boots were placed backward in the stirrups and a sword in its scabbard was strapped to the side. A caparisoned horse escorted army or marine colonels or above to their graves, one or more stars pinned to the blanket denoting a general.

As the commander-in-chief, the president also received a caparisoned horse, as had Abraham Lincoln in 1865. The animal today was more a dark chestnut than a jet black, and so handsome that the White House mistakenly identified him as Sardar, a stallion presented to Mrs. Kennedy by the president of Pakistan. In fact, he was Black Jack, a purely army horse. Foaled in Kansas, reared at Fort Reno in Oklahoma, the gelding bore the U.S. Army brand on his shoulder. One of the last horses ever issued by the quartermaster, he was sixteen years old and had served in the Old Guard for a decade.

Black Jack at the Capitol.

Black Jack's name honored General Pershing, who had acquired the nickname while commanding African-American troops in the southwest; as Pershing had risen in rank, the adjective had been changed to "black" from a bigoted and objectionable word. By sad coincidence, Black Jack had also been the nickname of Mrs. Kennedy's late father, flamboyant John V. Bouvier III.

The horse was the Brando of Fort Myer's stables, the alternate to a gentler animal whose name alone—Shorty—might have disqualified him from history. Sleek, dark, dangerous, a Morgan and quarter horse mix, Black Jack was an inspired choice of form over function. His hooves were so small that he was rarely ridden, but he was so striking that the role of the caparisoned horse suited him perfectly.

Historian Barbara W. Tuchman, who covered the funeral for the *St. Louis Post-Dispatch*, thought this animal was a perfect symbol for the late president, "constantly prancing in vigor, like the very word 'vigor' that had become, half in fun but with reason, his signature word."

Correspondent Nancy Dickerson of NBC News remembered Black Jack at the White House "rearing up on his hind legs so that the soldier had trouble controlling him. I was a little scared of him." The soldier was his nineteen-year-old reinsman, Private First Class Arthur A. Carlson of Robertsdale, Alabama. The stepson of a retired marine sergeant, Carlson had never worked with horses until being assigned to Black Jack ten months earlier. Now it was up to the Alabaman to control him.

The line of limousines trailed the caisson and the riderless horse and a large contingent of journalists walked behind the cars. The press had asked to participate in the procession to the Capitol, in fondness for the late president more than to collect news. Another contingent of police brought up the rear. Members of the White House staff gathered on the lawn to watch them go.

Sergeant Felder knew that Jack Kennedy had enjoyed the pomp and ceremony surrounding his office, had seen his grin on hearing *Hail to the Chief.* As the cortege stepped off toward the Capitol, Felder felt the president was "looking down on all this and reviewing it with approval."

"History saturates these pavements," ABC newsman Edward P. Morgan observed of Pennsylvania Avenue. Three hundred thousand people stood lining the sidewalks behind the honor cordon. They waited so quietly that some heard the click of traffic signals turning from red to green to yellow. Many were weeping. In the president's limousine, Lady Bird Johnson wanted to cry, too. The new first lady felt as though she was "moving, step by step, through a Greek tragedy."

What many of those waiting between the White House and the Capitol remembered most vividly later was what

Newsweek called "the doomsday echo of those drums." Nothing they had ever heard compared with it. Even experienced troops like new casket-team member Diamond were unprepared for the impact. The muffled drums were "the most impressive use of music" during the long weekend, a music historian later wrote, surpassing even famous compositions played during the funeral.

The custom traced back to the "magnificent funeral" in England for Major General Henry Ireton, Oliver Cromwell's son-in-law, in 1652. "Thus in a grave pace, drums covered with cloth, soldiers reversing their arms, they proceeded through the streets in a very solemn manner," wrote a contemporary diarist. In America, muffled drums wound through the presidential funerals of Lincoln, Garfield, William Henry Harrison, and Franklin Roosevelt.

There was no standard drum cadence in 1963 for a presidential cortege or for any military or state funeral. At Arlington, where small bands at military funerals often included only a single snare drum, army drummers played any solemn cadence they preferred. Master Sergeant Vincent Battista, principal drummer for the Army Band, generally played his own composition—a "very simple little short thing," he said later.

In a meeting at Fort Myer's auditorium on Saturday, Captain Mitchell asked Battista to demonstrate his cadence for assembled bandsmen. Almost by default, it became the president's cadence—and in the future, the standard beat for military funerals. Musicians noted that its tempo of a hundred beats per minute was about the cadence of a man's heart.

Robert Parker, a drummer in the Old Guard Fife and Drum Corps, remembered the notation decades later as Flam, Flam, Flam, 7 Stroke Roll—Flam, Flam, Flam, 7 Stroke Roll—Flam, Flam, Flam, 7 Stroke Roll—Flam,

Flam, Flam, Tap! To the nation, it sounded like this:

Boom, boom, boom, brmmmm.
Boom, boom, boom, brmmmm.
Boom, boom, boom, brmmmm.
Boom, boom, ba-boom!

Parker was among the army drummers selected for the joint detail. He felt he owed something to the president. Performing once at a White House reception, Parker had found himself standing four feet from John Kennedy. The president stood characteristically with hands in his jacket pockets, brothers Robert and Ted beside him.

Trying to be "extra sharp" during a passage in *The Downfall of Paris*, the young drummer had instead knocked himself in the forehead with a drumstick. The president quickly drew a hand from his jacket to hide his laughter. Ears burning and eyes watering, Bob Parker had kept drumming and never forgotten the small kindness. To be in the cortege now, he felt, was "quite an honor."

The cortege advanced up the empty avenue toward the Capitol. In streaming sunlight, the Associated Press said, it flowed through "canyons of mute staring faces, past the teen-agers clinging to statues and perched in the trees like starlings, past the grim gray government buildings with the flags at half staff and the doorways draped in black." A Washington secretary said later, "I felt like something went out of me when the casket went by."

At Pennsylvania and Tenth, opposite the Justice Department, a six-year-old girl from northwest Washington clutched a dozen red roses. Suddenly, Susie Bodrogi walked alone out into the middle of the street. No one watching from the sidewalk moved to retrieve her as she knelt and began arranging her flowers across the asphalt. She placed them one by one, then rose and hurried back to her parents

Master Sergeant Vincent Battista.

at the curbside. "The chill breeze pulled at the offering," *The Washington Post* noted, "but couldn't disturb it."

Troops stood at parade rest every twenty-five feet on both sides of the avenue. They didn't break formation or look around, but heard the people on the sidewalks behind them. The crowd was strangely quiet except for the low murmur of portable radios. These now began chattering about accused assassin Lee Harvey Oswald and Dallas police headquarters. "Someone shot that son of a bitch," a navy corpsman stationed in the crowd heard a man say.

The drums grew louder as the cortege approached Sergeant Gill, the marine from Cape Cod. The sound swelled so that "I could feel it pulsating, hitting my chest." It gave him goose bumps, but leathernecks like Gill learned in boot camp not to move or glance around in formation.

Every man in the cordon had orders to present arms when the caisson was exactly twelve steps away. Gill brought his rifle up with a slap and looked neither right nor left, only straight ahead toward the man doing the same across Pennsylvania Avenue. The cortege passed through his field of view.

"I saw the casket drawn by the horses," he recalled. "I could smell the horses—it was like in a stable. I could hear the wheels of the caisson creaking." It all made the president's death more real to the Massachusetts marine. Then the caisson trundled by "and there was the riderless horse." Black Jack was prancing and pulling on his reins—skittish, the newspapers all said.

The crowd now mistook the trailing journalists for ordinary citizens like themselves. Many left the curbs to join them, "as if they were hypnotized by the drums," said the *Boston Globe*. Police and marines with rifles and fixed bayonets formed a line to block their path at John Marshall Place, near the intersection of Pennsylvania and Constitution. But the rifles were carried at port arms and the confrontation was more confused than ugly; as the cortege drew nearer the Capitol, thousands of "other mourners" were allowed to fall in behind the police bringing up the rear of the column.

The procession arrived at the Capitol under a faultless sky at ten minutes before two. The drummers and escort troops marched past but the caisson halted in front of the east steps. It stopped in the wrong spot, but this was not enough to disrupt the ceremony. The family and mourners left the limousines, which departed. When everyone was in position, the Navy Band struck up *Ruffles and Flourishes.*

Ruffles are played on drums and flourishes simultaneously on bugles. The number of times they are sounded denotes the rank of the general or official present. The president received four ruffles and flourishes, the highest honor, immediately followed by *Hail to the Chief.* At Mrs. Kennedy's request, the musicians played at eighty-six beats per minute, dirge adagio. The familiar tune "sounded solemn rather than—as so many times when JFK had burst into a hall to its strains in the past—festive and exuberant," said *The Washington Post.* Mrs. Kennedy lowered her head and briefly appeared to fight tears.

The band then played *Eternal Father, Strong to Save,* which all sailors knew as the *Navy Hymn.* At the first note, the Third Infantry's salute battery began firing a twenty-one-gun salute at Louisiana Avenue and D Street near Union Station. The three artillery pieces were vintage three-inch antitank guns from World War II, refitted to fire seventy-five-millimeter blank shells. US ARMY was stenciled in white down their narrow barrels.

The gunners in dress blues were smooth and sure in their movements. The guns fired at five-second intervals timed by stopwatches; numbered cards tracked the sequence. The crash of guns rattled off buildings and echoed down the avenues, as if General Jubal Early and his rebel army had finally entered the federal capital a century after the Civil War.

As the big guns boomed, Lieutenant Bird's team unbuckled the casket from the caisson. General Wehle led the way up the wide steps, followed by the honor guard, and the

The casket team approaching the east steps.

national color detail. The body bearers with the casket were next. Seventy troops in a joint services honor cordon lined the steps. Thirty Kennedy aides and advisors formed a cordon of their own near the top.

Body bearers carry a casket about waist-high and from the side. Even for a team of eight, thirty-six marble steps presented a daunting obstacle. Sam Bird quickly realized his team was in trouble. Again, the lieutenant helped by grasping the casket himself. All the men could do was continue. Decades later, during President Reagan's funeral, a second casket team relieved the first on a landing midway up the much longer west steps. Bird's team ascended the east steps alone. About halfway, the lieutenant began to fear they wouldn't make it.

Moving the casket respectfully, Bird later wrote, took "every ounce of strength that all nine of us could muster." Quietly, the men urged each other on and somehow reached the top. In the pause before passing through the Capitol's great bronze doors, Lance Corporal Cheek noticed Sergeant Felder quivering from the effort.

A state funeral could make or break an army career, especially the honor guard company commander's, whose men represented the army and so were under intense scrutiny. No man in the Old Guard was under more emotional strain than Mike Groves. Felder considered his captain a "stickler for perfection and endurance," qualities that today counted for everything.

Groves and Lieutenant Bickley, the MDW media officer, watched with scores of officers and dignitaries as the body bearers entered the rotunda. The team's orders were not to carry the casket directly to the catafalque, but to circle the rotunda and approach from the west side. The men then had to step up onto the catafalque's base and settle the casket atop the black-draped bier.

The maneuver was difficult, but the captain trusted Felder. Their company football team had recently won the MDW championship; Groves was the center, his sergeant the quarterback. Felder later recalled that on the gridiron, the captain "followed my orders, knew his plays and was the most disciplined player on the team." Within the strictures of military life, they were friends.

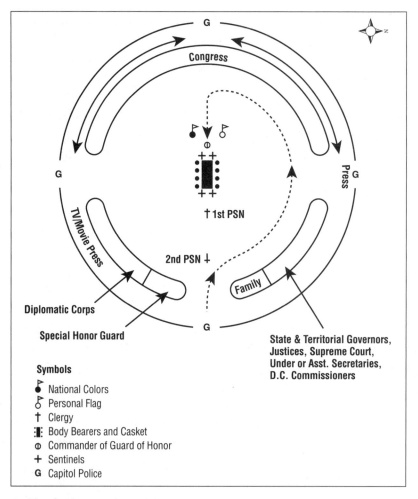

Plan for the rotunda service.

Inside the rotunda, the casket team passed within a few feet of the captain, who stood straight and impassive. The enormous physical strain was evident on Felder's face and on the others'. Lieutenant Bird still supported the head of the casket. Groves watched the men lower their burden into position. Felder and Mayfield then deftly straightened the draped American flag before they all stepped back.

Seaman Apprentice Nemuth had followed the casket into the rotunda with the presidential flag. The standard was so tall that he had to arch his back to pass through the doorway. The color bearers posted their flags in sturdy bases and stepped back, but the base for the presidential banner didn't fit. Nemuth held the flag in place throughout the ceremony, an improvisation many thought was planned. A relief death watch appeared from the west entrance and Bird and his team withdrew in their slow march.

The president's catafalque rested in the center of the circular room, America's nearest equivalent to Westminster Abbey. The fresco *Apotheosis of Washington* looked down from the canopy one hundred eighty feet above. The room's diameter was ninety-six feet of gleaming marble. Dignitaries stood shoulder-to-shoulder along the walls, the senate and house filling the western half of the chamber. The family stood opposite, near the massive painting *Landing of Columbus*. The cabinet, supreme court and U.S. delegates to the United Nations huddled beneath *Embarkation of the Pilgrims*. The White House staff and foreign delegations looked on near *Discovery of the Mississippi* and *Baptism of Pocahontas*.

The doorkeeper of the House, William "Fishbait" Miller, offered Adlai Stevenson a special place to stand. The United Nations ambassador and former presidential candidate just shook his head. A protestor had struck him with a sign during a recent visit to Dallas. Stevenson wished now that he had been killed there instead of the president.

Captain Pond, the Old Guard adjutant, had orders to assist the new president and the Kennedy family. When they arrived, Mrs. Kennedy asked him to remove her son, "John John," who would turn three on Monday. Then she changed her mind, saying, "No, let's see how long he can last."

During the eulogies, the boy began to glide his hands through the air as if flying an airplane. Pond looked to Mrs.

Kennedy, who acknowledged it was time for her son to go. A *Star* photographer captured the moment as the adjutant leaned down to the restless boy. The captain began to lead him away but was quickly stopped by the secret service.

"I was not going to give him up to someone I didn't know," Pond recalled. "But the secret service was not going to let me go anywhere with him." The captain took three or four steps before recognizing an agent and surrendering custody of the president's son.

Agents took John, Jr. to the speaker's office and gave him a miniature flag to play with. The boy asked them if he could have another "to take it home to my daddy."

Senate majority leader Michael J. Mansfield, Chief Justice Warren and Speaker of the House McCormack each delivered a short eulogy. While such addresses weren't unknown, says the army history, "neither were they a customary part of the lying in state ceremony." Although perfectly clear on television, odd acoustics made them almost inaudible in the rotunda itself. The Montana senator was the most piercing of the three speakers:

> There was a husband who asked much and gave much, and out of the giving and the asking wove with a woman what could not be broken in life, and in a moment it was no more. And so she took a ring from her finger and placed it in his hands, and kissed him and closed the lid of a coffin.

Some listeners found the eulogy too painful, almost harsh. Yet Mrs. Kennedy thought Mike Mansfield had struck just the right note. When he offered her his manuscript, she asked, "How did you know I wanted it?"

An Old Guard sergeant first class then helped Lyndon Johnson present a wreath. Allen J. "Mack" Eldredge was the ramrod-straight sergeant of the guard at the Tomb of

Mrs. Kennedy and children leaving the Capitol.

the Unknowns, a taut combat veteran regarded with awe within the unit. Eldredge walked the stand of carnations backwards to the casket and left the new president to linger there alone a moment and finger one of the flowers. Historian Manchester reported that the sergeant then broke down and was led away sobbing by two colonels.

The official ceremonies were concluded, but Mrs. Kennedy was reluctant to leave. Many of the young troops' regard for her husband extended equally to her. Casket-team member Jerry Diamond admired how she had tried to raise her family normally, knew that at leafy Camp David she had asked the guards to remain discretely at a distance. To a man, he recalled, the marines would "break our necks not to be seen. We really liked her."

Mrs. Kennedy went forward now with Caroline and

knelt beside the casket. The widow kissed the draped flag; her daughter's fingers slid beneath its red hem to caress the smooth wood. Body bearers and honor guards were trained to be impassive. But this, Jim Felder remembered, "was a very emotional moment for all of us." Men wearing decorations for valor had to look away. Some wept outright.

Then, mercifully, it was over. Leading a child with each hand, the former first lady walked back down the long steps and returned to the White House. On "this desperate day," Mrs. Johnson wrote, Mrs. Kennedy had achieved what had eluded her in the White House—"a state of love, a state of rapport between herself and the people of this country."

As if in proof, tens of thousands of strangers waited patiently in line outside the Capitol to pay their respects to her husband. "The Army men in their blue dress uniforms formed a great funnel from the door of the Capitol to the head of this long, long line" that extended out East Capitol Street, said the *Daily News*.

Within thirty minutes the line was twenty blocks long. It began moving through the rotunda at two o'clock and continued through the night.

ARLINGTON

Equipment operator Clifton Pollard had been eating breakfast in his Washington apartment Sunday morning when he received the phone call he had been expecting. Pollard was forty-two and had served with the army engineers in Burma during the war.

"Polly, could you please be here by eleven o'clock this morning?" his foreman asked. "I guess you know what it's for."

Pollard left for Arlington National Cemetery and met John Metzler at an equipment garage. The cemetery superintendent apologized for calling him in on a Sunday. Pollack replied that it was an honor to be there.

Jimmy Breslin of the New York *Herald Tribune* was also at Arlington. He had reported from Dallas earlier and was now covering the president's funeral. He watched Pollard use a reverse hoe—"a green machine with a yellow bucket"—to dig the president's grave at the bottom of the slope below the Custis-Lee mansion. Breslin also noted Pollard's pay rate—three dollars and one cent per hour.

In his *Herald Tribune* piece, he made it seem a lonely

affair, just Pollard, Metzler and another worker attending to the most basic task in a cemetery. But journalists and gawkers had also gathered. Cemetery workers erected makeshift walls of plywood and canvas to shield the scene and finished digging the grave with long-handled shovels. A photo taken from a helicopter appeared the next day in the *Post*.

Pollard saved some of the soil from the grave to fill in tracks he had left with his equipment. "I'd like to have everything, you know, nice," he told the New York reporter. The piece that ran in the *Herald Tribune* eventually appeared in journalism anthologies and helped establish Breslin's reputation. "I was just doing what we did in sports—," he said decades afterwards, "you talk with the loser."

The great concern through the weekend was protecting all the foreign dignitaries suddenly expected for the funeral on Monday. "This is the largest security problem we have ever faced," Police Chief Murray told reporters. With the nightmarish failure in Dallas on everyone's mind, vigilance remained extraordinarily high well into the coming week. Twenty-seven motorcycle escorts stood ready to shepherd motorcades from area airports to Washington hotels and embassies.

Already stretched thin, the DC police were soon over-extended; ninety-two percent of the nearly three thousand officers would be on duty during the funeral on Monday. But they wouldn't be on the streets alone. Chief Murray's force was joined by hundreds of agents from the defense department, FBI, CIA and secret service. The state department alone called in two hundred fifty plainclothes agents from offices around the country and set up a command post in its building at Twenty-first and Virginia, in Foggy Bottom, near the White House. Plus, many foreign embassies had their own security forces, which were augmented by agents who accompanied dignitaries into the country.

The reinforcements also included three hundred military police from the District of Columbia national guard and two hundred national park service police. Twenty-eight officers from New York City paid their way down to Washington, hoping to form an honor guard at St. Matthew's Cathedral. "We came down here to pay our respects to the president," said an NYPD patrolmen. "When we got here, the Washington police asked us to give them a hand. The crowds were more than they expected."

The volunteer agencies were also out in force. Two hundred sixty-five Red Cross emergency workers offered first aid in and near the Capitol. Thirty Salvation Army volunteers operated a canteen to feed police and troops on the streets. No one totaled the military, law enforcement and civilian personnel involved, but it surely exceeded ten thousand. The military alone contributed nearly seven thousand troops during the four days.

Small incidents appeared large. Sunday afternoon, a traffic officer thought he saw the stock of a rifle in a passing car. Dispatchers put out a description of five men in a blue Ford; the report was picked up by radio and television. When the car was pulled over, the occupants were college students who had driven down from New York. Police cited the driver for improper license plates.

With immense crowds gathering around the Capitol, sixty children ranging in age from six to sixteen got separated from their parents by early evening. From the district and five states, they all wound up at police headquarters in the roll call room of the women's bureau. Jail matrons kept them occupied until their parents appeared.

Women officers also had a tangential connection to the assassination. Judge Hughes, who had administered the oath of office to Lyndon Johnson on board Air Force One, was a former colleague. Forty years earlier, she had worked on the metropolitan force during the day while attending George Washington University law school at night.

Sunday afternoon, a new "Mrs. Kennedy requests . . ." reached the Pentagon. The widow wanted an "eternal flame" at the president's graveside, like one she had seen at the Arc de Triomphe in 1961. Mrs. Kennedy had so wowed the French during that visit that the president had introduced himself as "the man who accompanied Jacqueline Kennedy to Paris," a quip he had repeated in Texas. Perhaps that explained why his widow's thoughts turned to Paris; she later told historian Manchester that the eternal flame "just came into my head."

A call went out to Lieutenant General Walter K. Wilson Jr., head of the army corps of engineers. Somewhere, Mrs. Kennedy's request got embellished, and someone tried to tell General Wilson that the flame should constantly shift colors. That was too much for the corps commander. "We're going to have a one-colored flame," Wilson snapped. "We're not going to make a Coney Island out of this thing."

The corps normally handled massive construction projects such as dams and river locks. Responsibility for the symbolic little flame filtered down to a pair of field officers: Colonel Clayton B. Lyle Jr., head of the corps' utilities division, and Lieutenant Colonel Bernard G. Carroll Jr., Fort Myer's post engineer.

Lyle was at home watching televised news coverage when his phone rang. "We've got a problem," General Wilson said. The eternal flame had to be ready at the president's grave by eight o'clock the next morning. Wilson told Lyle, "You've got the job." Carroll was already sitting in Jack Metzler's office at Arlington when his call came. "There was no panic," Carroll recalled twenty years later. "There was a sense of having a job to do and having to get things done . . . in a hurry."

Both men were experienced engineers. Lyle had built everything from roads to radar stations on assignments from Europe to Guam. Carroll had piloted a B-25 while commanding a weather station in North Africa, then had earned the Legion of Merit in Korea for helping renovate the port of Inchon. More impressive to some was that Carroll's baseball teammate in high school was the great Ted Williams.

The two engineers coordinated their efforts. Lyle's team met at the engineer school at Fort Belvoir outside Washington to design and fabricate a lamp. Carroll and his men at Fort Myer took charge of assembling a fuel system. The project would have been easy except for the timing. The few hours remaining, Wilson said, "really put us in the middle of things."

In Virginia, Colonel Lyle made quick sketches of what an eternal flame might look like. The main component was a luau lamp, the kind used for outdoor parties, with metal strips welded on to support the frame. General Wilson remembered the engineers designing it "right on the floor there" at Fort Belvoir. The school's troops then began the fabrication under Sergeant First Class Leon Canfield, a welding instructor, later killed in a bulldozer accident in South Vietnam.

Once the lamp was ready, the troops tested the flame with water and blasts of air to ensure that normal weather conditions wouldn't douse it. Tapers for lighting it were fashioned from welding rods and pieces of gun cloth.

At Fort Myer, Colonel Carroll lacked the proper materials to build a pipeline. He started calling hardware stores in suburban Virginia and Maryland, hoping to locate copper tubing and bottled propane. Nearly every business that might have been open on a normal Sunday was closed in mourning. After an hour with the yellow pages, the engineer reached a repairman at Suburban Propane in Rockville, Maryland. Carroll explained the situation.

The repairman was headed out on an emergency call, but said, "I'll be glad to get you anything you want." He had someone deliver the materials to the army.

Late that night, the two army teams met on the hillside at Arlington. Colonel Lyle's men installed their luau lamp. With no time to lay a permanent gas pipeline, Colonel Carroll's men dug a narrow trench for a one-inch pipe connected to a tank of propane, which they concealed behind shrubs three hundred feet higher up the slope. The whole system was so hastily rigged that the secret service later worried about safety.

The engineers tested their apparatus in the early hours of Monday. General Wilson personally supervised tests to determine how long it took the gas to flow down the line after a valve was opened. "At the right moment, we signaled a man at the tank to turn it on," Lyle recalled. The lamp worked perfectly. Satisfied, Wilson gazed about at the gravesite. It was a beautiful location, he thought, and "helped ease the pain."

The state department hadn't planned to invite foreign leaders to the funeral, feeling that time was too short for invitations and travel. But it had misjudged the depth of the sorrow overseas. By Saturday, American ambassadors were cabling Washington that this head of state or that monarch wished to attend the services. Various dignitaries—most notably President Charles de Gaulle, that prickly but gallant French ally—then said they would sidestep protocol and come as private citizens. De Gaulle later declared that he had been "sent by the people of France."

The department "hastily cabled formal invitations," wrote Mossman and Stark. "A flood of acceptances followed." Among nearly a hundred foreign dignitaries, the *New York Times* counted twelve royals, eighteen republican heads of state, thirty-four foreign ministers, six vice premiers or vice presidents and two former presidents.

Even the United Nations had never seen such an assemblage: Emperor Haile Selassie of Ethiopia, the "Lion of Judah"; Prince Philip and Prime Minister Alec Douglas-Home of Great Britain; Queen Frederika of Greece and King Baudouin of Belgium; Chancellor Ludwig Erhard of West Germany and Mayor Willy Brandt of Berlin; Japan's Crown Prince Akihito and Prince Harald of Norway; Deputy Premier Anastas Mikoyan of the Soviet Union; and dozens more. Newspaper lists ran multiple columns.

When the leaders began arriving on Sunday, it was left to the air traffic controllers to decide whose planes took priority in landing at Dulles International, National, Friendship and Andrews airports. Secretary of State Dean Rusk arrived at Dulles at four forty-five Sunday afternoon and stayed until late evening, shuttling from gate to gate. Undersecretary W. Averell Harriman and assistant secretaries did the same there and the other airfields.

Among the first to arrive was President de Gaulle, himself the target of several assassination attempts. Security was heavy at futuristic Dulles. "A crowd of a few hundred stood quietly watching through the afternoon and evening hours," the *Star* reported. Arrivals were often delayed "as the huge mobile lounges shuttled from runway to terminal gates and back."

One international figure didn't arrive and likely wouldn't have been received if she had. Ngo Dinh Nhu was the beautiful and divisive former "first lady" of South Vietnam, a role she had played for her unmarried brother-in-law, President Ngo Dinh Diem. On November 2, Diem and his brother, Madame Nhu's husband, had been assassinated in an American-sanctioned coup. From Rome, the deposed "Dragon Lady" drafted a chilling message to Mrs. Kennedy and on Sunday released it to the press.

She expressed "profound sympathy" for the family, while observing with exquisite cruelty that "anything happening in Vietnam will surely find equivalence in the U.S.A." She added that Mrs. Kennedy's loss "might seem to you even more unbearable because of your habitually well-sheltered life."

Madame Nhu—who had infamously dismissed the self-immolation of Buddhist monks protesting her husband's regime as "barbecues"—bitterly noted that "the wounds inflicted on President Kennedy were identical to those of President Ngo Dinh Diem, and of my husband." She ended by assuring her newly widowed counterpart that "our most sincere thoughts and prayers are with you and your dear ones." The *Chicago Daily News* called it "barbed sympathy."

Uncounted thousands of Americans also descended on the capital, many driving into the district from nearby states as early as Saturday. Authorities had planned to close the rotunda at nine o'clock, but the line of mourners waiting to pass the catafalque grew so quickly that they decided to keep the Capitol open all night.

It was the largest crowd one metropolitan police sergeant had seen in more than twenty years on the force. "Where are they all coming from?" another sergeant wondered. "Midnight," said *The Times* of London, "was meaningless."

One family of four drove down from Orange, New Jersey. The father was fortunate to find a motel near the cemetery.

Attempting to drive to the Capitol Sunday night, however, he lost his way and stopped for directions at a small guardhouse downtown. "Say, fella, do you have any idea where you are?" asked a sympathetic police captain at the White House.

By the time the family had parked and reached the Capitol, each parent carrying a child, the line to enter the rotunda was inconceivably long. It extended dozens of blocks and doubled back on itself. A Missouri congressman who drove it at eleven o'clock reported the total length as nine miles and the Boston *Globe* agreed. Most estimates were shorter, but still measured in miles.

The wait took hours. The family from Orange returned to their motel to await the funeral procession on Monday. "There is no way of speeding up the line of people filing by," said NBC's Robert Abernethy in the rotunda. "Everybody seems to want to linger." Jim Felder, who passed the line early the next morning on his way to Fort Myer, thought it would have "impressed the devil himself."

Mrs. Kennedy visited the rotunda with Robert Kennedy shortly after nine o'clock Sunday night, at "a merciful moment when the TV cameras were by chance searching elsewhere," according to the *Washington Daily News*. The line of mourners stopped and pressed against the ropes as she went forward to the casket and knelt. The thirty-four-year-old widow prayed for about two minutes, then rose and left as quietly as she had entered.

A woman recognized her and offered a silent embrace. Mrs. Kennedy returned it. Outside again, she said to her brother-in-law, "Let's walk a bit." Coatless, she walked west on Constitution Avenue in the cold night air, trailed by a policeman and a clutch of reporters. She paused to exchange a few words with a group of Sisters of Mercy, whose mother offered condolences. Reporter Mary McGrory later remembered the president's quip that bishops and monsignors were always Republicans, but "sisters were inevitably Democratic."

Someone asked the attorney general about the vast congregation that had come for his brother. "Fantastic," Robert Kennedy murmured, "fantastic."

A crowd began to gather and after fifteen minutes the president's widow had walked enough. "Perhaps the memories came crowding too much, perhaps the uselessness of this last visit became apparent," speculated *The Times*. Mrs. Kennedy stepped into her car with the attorney general and glided off to the White House.

People kept joining the line as the temperature slipped past freezing. Among them was former world heavyweight boxing champion "Jersey Joe" Wolcott. He had driven down to Washington from his home and waited nine hours to walk past the catafalque. Wolcott said afterwards of the president, "He was a great man."

By midnight, the police began warning that the line was too long for everyone to view the casket before the rotunda closed at nine a.m. They repeated the warning hourly through the small hours; but, an officer said, people "just wouldn't believe us." At the Statler Hilton, guests checked in but didn't use their rooms. Everyone was on the line, which was orderly and eerily quiet. Someone later recalled "Americans weeping softly before me and behind me. No one talked."

When they finally reached the Capitol, mourners climbed the east steps and moved to the left or the right as they entered the rotunda. The lines passed on both sides of the casket, then went out to the west steps and the mall. No one attempted to count them all. Estimates ran as high as a quarter-million.

Inside, nearly the only sound was the squeak of soles on

Mourners waiting to enter the Capitol.

the marble floor. Many made the sign of the cross. Servicemen stopped and saluted and went quietly on. The *Star* also noted the gentleness of the police, who escorted blind mourners with "a hand on the arm and a soft voice description of the casket and its guards." To an elderly woman who lingered too long, an officer said, "You'll have to move along, ma'am. I'm sorry. I'm really sorry."

Barbara Tuchman, however, was unawed. The rotunda was bright as "a television rehearsal studio"; the death watch was "nervous and very young." Only the crowd impressed her, "almost entirely under 40, with teenagers and families with young children. In them was the significance of the occasion. This funeral belonged to them."

Late Sunday night, Sam Bird and his eight body bearers went out to Arlington to prepare for Monday. After their ordeal that afternoon, the lieutenant wanted to reassure his men they could carry the casket down the Capitol steps without incident, again at St. Matthew's, and finally at the burial in Arlington.

After inspecting the church, he had recommended using a church truck to transport the casket up the long aisle to the services. He didn't learn the suggestion was approved until Monday.

The team couldn't practice at the Capitol, so the steps leading to the Tomb of the Unknowns had to do. A regulation army casket filled with sandbags substituted for the president's. Bird ordered his team repeatedly to carry the casket up and down the steps. Worried that the casket wasn't heavy enough, he had two tomb sentinels sit atop it when they went off duty at midnight. The body bearers carried it up and down as if running people out of town on a rail.

The punishing drill did not go well, but grew macabre and worrying—"kind of comical," Staff Sergeant Gaudreau thought. No one wanted to allow the president's casket to slip or tilt tomorrow. To let it drop was unthinkable. Bird continued until nearly one o'clock before finally calling a halt.

"Don't worry, fellas," he said. "The adrenaline will get flowing. We'll get it done." Despite the rough night, Diamond recalled, Bird appeared confident and so "instilled confidence in us." The body bearers took a brief rest, then returned at five a.m. to rehearse at the graveside for another two hours.

MDW headquarters distributed the final funeral plans to all commands and agencies involved on Sunday evening. General Wehle's last briefing for military commanders and agency representatives stretched into early Monday. "This will be as close to a combat situation as some of you may ever get," he had barked at the beginning of the exhausting weekend. Wehle was right about the current pressures, but for many of his officers wrong about their prospects for combat.

Around two a.m., someone asked about the bugler. Men just looked at one another. Somehow, this essential detail of any military funeral—a bugler to sound Taps—had been forgotten. Despite the bedeviled hour, a call was placed to the home of Keith Clark, the principal bugler of the U.S. Army Band.

Clark was a unique soldier. A specialist sixth class— a rank later abolished, equivalent to staff sergeant—he was addressed as Sergeant Clark. Unlike most troops, the bugler's duties hadn't been assigned at random. Clark had graduated from Michigan's prestigious Interlochen Music School and played trumpet in the Grand Rapids Symphony. Even the army didn't waste such talent. After seventeen years in uniform—"musicians first and soldiers second," he later said of the band—Clark now held perhaps the best military job in Washington.

Lost in his home library of antiquarian books, he hadn't heard of the president's death for some hours on Friday. When the news broke through at last, Clark had hurried out for a haircut. The predawn call now, a day and a half later, was no more unexpected than Pollard's.

Clark later was the model for a minor character in *Gardens of Stone*; "the best lip on the post," the novel called him. Such a nod in fiction was fitting. Like Private Robert E. Lee Prewitt in another army novel, James Jones' *From Here to Eternity*, Clark was good—"good enough to play the Armistice Day Taps at Arlington, the Mecca of all Army buglers. He really had a call."

To ex-soldier Jones, Taps represented "the Great Loneliness," and soldiers who heard it felt "suddenly very near the man beside them, who also was a soldier, who also must die." Montgomery Clift had movingly recreated such a moment in the movie.

But Clift was only an actor and Keith Clark was a genuine army bugler. He really had sounded Taps for the president—just two weeks earlier on Armistice Day. In a few hours, he would do it again.

MONDAY
NOVEMBER 25

MONDAY, NOVEMBER 25

CATHEDRAL

The day was again fine and cold for the president—"as crisp and clear as one of his own instructions," wrote Mary McGrory. Lieutenant Sam Bird arrived at the Capitol with his body bearers a little after ten o'clock and gathered the men around him in an alcove off the rotunda. He asked them to bow their heads.

"Dear God," he prayed, "please give us strength to do this last thing for the president."

Their heads came up and Bird checked his watch.

"Let's move," he said.

The team had been scheduled to relieve the death watch and take the casket at ten twenty-seven. But the family was late arriving, then asked for a final moment alone at the bier. Mrs. Kennedy prayed with brothers-in-law Robert and Ted for about ten minutes. The team rigidly held its position and waited. Finally, the family rose and departed. The site control officer, an Old Guard captain, solemnly nodded to Bird. It was nearly eleven o'clock when the lieutenant gave his order.

"Secure casket!"

The body bearers executed their slow-motion ballet, lifting the casket from the catafalque and carrying it out through the east entrance's tall bronze doors. They had dampened their white cotton gloves to improve their grip on the handles. Outside, they paused at the top of the steps as troops below presented arms.

"Don't fail me now," marine Jerry Diamond silently told himself. "You don't want to be the one who locked knees and passed out."

Platoon Sergeant Jesse Sharp briefly joined the team as the Coast Guard Band played *Ruffles and Flourishes* and *Hail to the Chief.* The Old Guard sergeant held the foot of the casket while Bird held the head. This gave the body bearers each a final moment to loosen his grip and flex his arms. Then they started down the steps as the band began *O God of Loveliness.*

The dread everyone had felt quickly vanished. The body bearers carried the flag-draped casket into the sunlight, a biographer wrote, "as though the weight had been taken out of their hands." Sergeant Felder remembered the passage as "a perfect execution of military precision." A breeze ruffled the flag at the bottom of the steps. Felder and Lance Corporal Cheek each freed a hand to smooth it down atop the casket.

"We got it down the steps no problem," the sergeant remembered a quarter-century later, "breathed a sigh of relief, and put it on the caisson."

When the caisson started off to the White House, Bird and his men stood and watched it go. They had much to do yet today and the army had spared them the march to St. Matthew's. They walked off to a waiting bus, which they rode standing up to preserve the perfect creases in their uniforms.

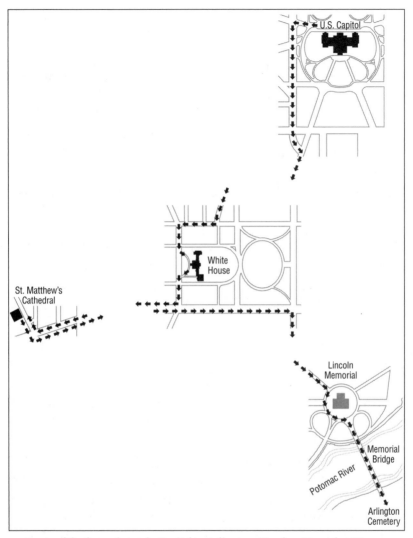

Route of the funeral march, Capitol to Arlington, Monday, November 25.

The march route to Arlington National Cemetery had three distinct segments, punctuated by pauses: the Capitol to the White House, the mansion to St. Matthew's, the cathedral to the cemetery. The overall distance was what *The Washington Post* called a "five-mile lane of sorrow."

A police chief and four of his staff led the way. Then came General Wehle, followed by the commander of troops, Lieutenant Colonel Richard E. Cross of the Third Infantry. Marching behind them were three large march units and then the cortege. The march units totaled twenty companies, squadrons and bands, plus one platoon. These represented every branch of the armed forces and reserves, plus veterans of these forces.

Bands from all five services participated today, but only three (and the Black Watch pipers) marched in the procession. The army was the senior service and its band normally would have led the first unit. Mrs. Kennedy, however, asked for the scarlet-coated Marine Band. The Army Band was scheduled to play instead at St. Matthew's, as the Coast Guard Band had done at the Capitol. Also by special request, the Old Guard Fife and Drum Corps in its colonial uniforms were to greet the cortege at Arlington, but not perform there. The Air Force Pipe Band would participate at the gravesite.

Next behind the Marine Band came a company of cadets from the Military Academy at West Point. Their long gray lines, Russell Baker wrote in the *Times*, marched with "a precision to break a drill sergeant's heart." Another reporter who watched them pass wondered in later years how many of them had survived the war in Vietnam. Following the cadets came the companies from the naval, air force and coast guard academies.

Behind the cadets and midshipmen came companies of active-duty soldiers, sailors, airmen and coasties; the army company came from the Old Guard. Behind these units, which were all male, marched a composite company of uniformed servicewomen.

Women had served in the military since World War II and briefly in the war before that. They nonetheless belonged to separate organizations such as the navy WAVES (Women Accepted for Volunteer Emergency Service) and army WACs (Women's Army Corps). They wouldn't fully integrate into the armed forces and bands until the middle nineteen-seventies. But including a company of women in the procession under the command of a WAC major wasn't an afterthought or another request by Mrs. Kennedy—there was ample precedent.

WAVES had marched in the procession for President Franklin Roosevelt in 1945; first lady Eleanor Roosevelt had supported women in the war and FDR had once served as an assistant navy secretary. A mixed company of women later marched in the cortege for the chief of naval operations in 1951. It included platoons of WAVES, WACs, WAFs (Women in the Air Force) and Women Marines. (Few coast guard women, called SPARS, served at that time.) Noting the navy's example, the army included a composite company in the 1955 funeral for a retired chief of staff.

So servicewomen, too, participated in the president's procession—bringing up the rear of the first march unit, under the command of an army major. The company had never marched together before today. Despite temperatures that wouldn't exceed fifty, the women stepped off without overcoats, as did the men.

Navy Lieutenant Jo Oberg had learned she would lead the WAVE platoon at ten-thirty Sunday night. One of her troops was a navy legend, among the first women to enlist during World War II. Oberg thought the servicewomen "would have looked better as separate units," but felt honored to take part. She later concluded, "We marched pretty well for not having any practice together."

Minority troops were better represented. Segregation in the armed forces had ended by order of President Truman in 1948. Change was sometimes slow in elite units; Jim

Felder was among the first ten African Americans in the Old Guard. Many thought the late president, too, had been slow to address civil rights. But at his inauguration in 1961, he had pointedly noted an all-white unit marching in the parade. The Pentagon got the message. On this brittle afternoon a thousand days later, Sergeant Felder (with Seaman Apprentice Clark) was a highly visible African-American presence at the casket—and Felder had been selected for his experience, not his race.

The *New York Times* observed that there were African Americans in each unit in the procession—a symbol, it said, "of Mr. Kennedy's commitment against racial discrimination." *The Times* of London even noted in the Air Force Pipe Band an African American, "wearing the kilt, at the big drum."

The Navy Band led the second march unit, which included companies and squadrons representing all the reserve and national guard forces. The Air Force Band led the third unit, comprising representatives of twenty-two veterans' organizations (including two military mothers' groups), the special forces platoon from Fort Bragg, and a marine company. The positioning of the green berets and marines came at the request of the family.

The cortege, as it had the day before, included the joint chiefs, color guard, caisson, caparisoned horse and presidential flag bearer. Absent were the body bearers, who were marching today only from St. Matthew's to Arlington. During the first segment to the White House, the family rode in limousines and a police escort once more brought up the rear.

In other world capitals, generals, field marshals and admirals would have escorted a slain leader to his grave. The president's cortege had no lack of brass or braid, but great responsibility also fell to enlisted men and junior officers. A major general might command the column, with the be-ribboned joint chiefs of staff striding a few paces ahead of the caisson. But ordinary troops—some fresh from boot camp or basic training—bore the casket and shouldered the rifles. They carried the flags and led the restless horse, blew the bugle and beat the drums. They marched through cordons of citizens just like themselves. This had always been the way in the American military.

The crowds along the sidewalks were much larger than Sunday's. A million mourners stood ten and twelve deep from the Capitol to the White House, then to the cathedral, and on across the Potomac to the cemetery, newspapers reported. It was mostly "a silent crowd, a crowd of bowed heads and tears," said the *Evening Star*. Millions more watched from home, transfixed by black-and-white television. The country simply stopped. "John F. Kennedy's casket did not ride down Pennsylvania Avenue only," *Newsweek* observed. "It rode down Main Street."

Twelve hundred troops lined both sides of the march route from the Capitol to the cathedral. After the procession had passed, those closest to Capitol Hill crossed town on buses to extend the cordon down past the Lincoln Memorial and over the bridge into Virginia.

The drummers from yesterday had rejoined their bands. Today, the troops marched not only to the muffled drums but also to funeral music and hymns. Each band leading a march unit had three pieces of music to play. These ranged from *America the Beautiful* and hymns to funeral marches by Chopin and Beethoven. The bands had scrambled to find all the sheet music, sharing the contents of their libraries with each other. They would play the same pieces on the march from the cathedral to the cemetery.

The caisson leaving the White House on Monday.

Private First Class Richard A. Pace of Marion, Indiana, rode one of the big grays pulling the caisson. He tried to look dignified and gaze past the people lining the sidewalks. The soldiers rode together without any crisp orders to set the tempo. "There were no commands given," Pace remembered long afterward. "We did it all by instinct. Nobody said a word."

Behind the trundling caisson, the caparisoned horse pranced and shied, noticeably more skittish than on Sunday. To one television reviewer, it was as if "everything he had to do was distasteful to him." Private Carlson told the newspapers later that Black Jack was merely proud, but the crowds and perhaps transmitted emotion had made the animal wild. He was sweating and barely controllable.

Years later, Carlson admitted that Black Jack "had never behaved like that before. He kept throwing his head. I was thinking, 'What am I going to do if my arm wears out and he gets away from me?'"

Yet to anyone watching, the procession appeared beautifully orchestrated as it moved away from the Capitol. The most affecting music was the Air Force Band's rendition of Chopin's funeral march—the slow *tum-tum-ta-tum* playfully hummed or whistled in so many American movies, cartoons and schoolrooms. Hearing it played now in earnest, perhaps for the first time, struck like a slap.

All eyes and cameras followed the caisson. With no escorts marching beside it and only Nemuth with his flag trailing behind, the draped casket looked stark and solitary. "There is nothing quite so moving as the sight of horses pulling a wooden wagon," observed NBC's David Brinkley. As the cortege continued up Pennsylvania Avenue, *The Washington Post* said, the "steady beat and roll of drums blended with the tolling of St. John's church as it drew near the mansion."

The units marching in front of the cortege continued past the White House, turned right on Seventeenth Street, NW, and stopped facing north. A platoon from the marine company at the rear of the third march unit peeled off to turn left and led the cortege in through the mansion's northeast gate. Mrs. Kennedy wanted marines to escort the president onto the grounds and this unique maneuver was the only way to free up the men; every marine "between Philadelphia and Quantico with a set of dress blues," an officer recalled, was already involved in the procession or honor cordons.

The Naval Academy Catholic Choir sang *Londonderry Air*

and the *Navy Hymn* quietly on the White House lawn as the Black Watch pipers fell in behind the marines. The cortege paused a few minutes on the grounds before continuing. The family left the limousines while the foreign dignitaries assembled on the north drive to walk together to St. Matthews. Again, this was Mrs. Kennedy's inspiration, announced on Saturday evening.

Chief of protocol Angier Biddle Duke had the delicate duty of readying the dignitaries. "I asked the chiefs of state to step forward, and to my intense, amazed relief they all fit in one line across the north driveway," he recalled. "I wanted them all to march in equal rank, and, by God, they did."

Tom Wicker of the *New York Times* noticed "President de Gaulle in the uniform and cap of the French Army, the diminutive Haile Selassie in gorgeous braid, Prince Philip in the blue of the Royal Navy, others in top hats, sashes, medals, or simple civilian clothes like those worn by Queen Frederika."

The ranks behind them looked more precise on paper than they would on Seventeenth Street, but it hardly mattered. The family was to walk behind the cortege and caparisoned horse. Then came the president and Mrs. Johnson; children Caroline and John in a limousine; the foreign delegations; supreme court justices; cabinet members; members of congress; presidential assistants; personal friends; and, at Mrs. Kennedy's invitation, members of the White House staff.

President Johnson had heard the pleas to travel the eight blocks to the cathedral in an enclosed car. Since Dallas, many serious people considered it madness to let a president walk exposed on an American street. The new commander-in-chief earthily rejected the counsel. He would go on foot with the others. The next day, Mrs. Kennedy wrote to thank him for several kindnesses, including walking "behind Jack."

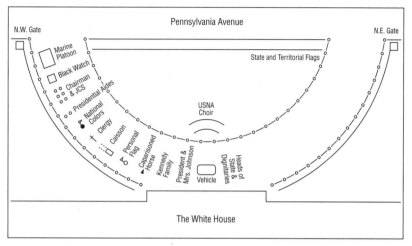

Plan for the cortege at the White House.

Mrs. Kennedy stepped off for St. Matthew's at eleven-forty as the Black Watch pipers began *The Brown Haired Maiden.* Her brothers-in-law walked on each side, Robert on her right, Edward to her left. The procession and cortege would march north along Seventeenth Street onto Connecticut Avenue. It was the largest gathering of presidents, royalty and prime ministers since the funeral of King Edward VII in London in 1910.

More than fifty guards and detectives walked among the politicians and dignitaries and many others stood wary watch along the curbs and on the rooftops. Captain Mitchell of the Army Band watched Mrs. Kennedy and the new president depart from near the White House gate. Acutely conscious of all the security keyed to sudden movements, he delivered "the slowest salute of my life."

Historian Barbara Tuchman, who had opened her acclaimed *The Guns of August* with a description of the Edward's epoch-ending funeral, found the informality shocking. "No plumes, no horses that in another era gave dignitaries that necessary extra stature to lift them above their fellow men," she wrote, "—just men and women walking together in a group." But, she added, it "was not, after all, their day."

The day was Mrs. Kennedy's. Nothing in her history had prepared her for marching. The attorney general had been a sailor at the end of World War II, but brother Ted had never served in the armed forces. Yet, with Mrs. Kennedy leading, they all strode together in step and in time to the pipers skirling *The Badge of Scotland*, *The 51st Highland Division* and *The Barren Rocks of Aden*.

"Deeply veiled and with unfaltering step, she strode up Connecticut with head and shoulders erect, looking neither left nor right, marching at a soldier's pace," Baker wrote. The kings, princes and presidents behind her, *The New Yorker* added, "strode down a sunlit street like a grim village rabble; and Jacqueline Kennedy became Persephone, the Queen of Hades and the beautiful bride of grief."

It was as if the young widow had trained all her life for this moment. No Hollywood or Broadway actress had ever created a scene so affecting. Chief Justice Warren, who walked in the procession, later wrote, "I could not understand how she stood it."

Green-domed St. Matthew's was the family's local parish, "a small edifice of red brick, granite, and sandstone," the *Globe* told New England. Almost homely outside, inside it had a high altar of white marble carved in India and impressive mosaics of Matthew, Mark, Luke and John. Its ten-foot center doors were draped today in gold and black bunting.

The march units came north between the modern financial buildings lining Seventeenth, curved onto Connecticut, passed the Mayflower and various fine stores and antiques shops, then turned east onto Rhode Island Avenue.

*Mrs. Kennedy, with Robert and Edward Kennedy, leads the march to
St. Matthew's.*

They marched past St. Matthew's and made three turns on
an irregular block before stopping on Connecticut, facing
south.

As at the Capitol, the caisson stopped when it came abreast
of the steps. Without pausing, Mrs. Kennedy led the dignitaries through an honor cordon and into the cathedral.
Those guests who hadn't come with her, including Presidents Truman and Eisenhower and President Hoover's two
sons, were already seated inside. The Black Watch and the
veterans groups left the formation and Sam Bird's body
bearers returned.

The Army Band played *Ruffles and Flourishes* and *Hail to the Chief,* followed by *Pray for the Dead.* Sergeant Felder and the body bearers unstrapped the casket during the hymn and lifted it from the caisson about ten past noon. A young woman from Boston, watching from across the street, later said, "It suddenly became very cold and very quiet."

The body bearers started forward, but Richard Cardinal Cushing of Boston startled them by coming to the bottom of the steps to bless the casket. Lieutenant Bird was forced to halt his team in the street. Again, he stepped forward to grip the casket himself. In the dry understatement of army historians Mossman and Stark, the team held its position "only with difficulty." Bird was ready to whisper, "Sir, you'd better move!" when the cardinal completed his blessing.

The team again moved slowly up the steps—the men "seem to be bearing the weight of the world," said *TV Guide*—and finally entered the cathedral. Nemuth remained outside with the presidential flag. The units out on Connecticut Avenue stood "at ease" and shivered in the shadows. A small dog dashed up the cathedral steps as a dirge sounded inside. A police officer shooed it away.

The Old Guard had diplomatically but firmly ejected parishioners from the eight o'clock mass who had attempted to remain for the president's. His was a low mass, less elaborate than a high mass, conducted by Cardinal Cushing and Auxiliary Bishop Philip N. Hannan of Washington. The cardinal had presided at the president's wedding and the burial of his son Patrick. Hannan, a former paratrooper and family friend, participated instead of his archbishop at Mrs. Kennedy's request. Tenor Luigi Vena, choir director of a church in Massachusetts, today sang with the cathedral choir; he, too, had taken part in her wedding.

Fifty-eight military officers wearing black armbands served as ushers. Twelve hundred mourners with color-coded, numbered invitations occupied all twenty-seven rows of pews and every temporary seat. Among the last to arrive were the Reverend Martin Luther King and Mary Ryan, a diminutive nurse and distant Irish relative of the president's; Pan Am had rushed her over from Shannon at the last instant.

Wanting to follow protocol, Bishop Hannan had asked for a list of the dignitaries. He had met a state department official in the sacristy at ten-thirty, only to learn that the diplomats were overwhelmed. "We haven't kept any list," the man admitted. "So many came that we didn't know were coming." He advised the bishop to stand up front and "just watch the chief guests" as they entered the cathedral.

Outside in the shadows and chilly sunshine, the march units stood and waited. Portable latrines had been left in the wrong location and most troops couldn't take a relief break. Lieutenant Oberg and her servicewomen met "a very obliging man" who let them use the facilities in an old building nearby.

The hour-long mass was a simple one of hymns and prayers recited in Latin, spoken rather than sung, "not unlike any other celebrated daily by Catholic priests," said the *Star*. Except that this mass was celebrated by a cardinal with the face and voice of "a great craggy archangel," in the words of a later David Wolper documentary. Sunlight bathed the altar.

There were no eulogies afterwards. Bishop Hannan began a simple eleven-minute homily in English by reading passages from scripture. He followed with brief excerpts from the president's inaugural address, including the famous exhortation:

And so, my fellow Americans, ask not what your country can do for you; ask what you can do for your country.

Cardinal Cushing then circled the casket, sprinkling holy water and wafting incense to bestow final absolution. "When you have known a man since childhood," said the *Boston Globe*, "have performed his marriage ceremony and baptized his children, you think of him first as a human being." The night before, the sixty-eight-year-old cardinal had wept during a nationally televised mass from Boston. At St. Matthew's, he recited another prayer in Latin, which was unfamiliar to many in the church and millions watching on television. Then, in a brilliant, spontaneous moment, the cardinal broke into English.

"May the angels, dear Jack, lead you into Paradise. May the martyrs receive you at your coming. May the spirit of God embrace you, and mayest thou, with all those who made the supreme sacrifice of dying for others, receive eternal rest and peace. Amen."

Mrs. Kennedy briefly wept as she left St. Matthew's. Caroline, as she had at other moments through the weekend, put her hands over her mother's, trying to comfort her. Poet Wendell Berry captured the scene.

> . . . *we know his death's horses and drums; the roses, bells, candles, crosses; the faces hidden in veils* . . .

The cardinal noticed mother and daughter standing together outside. Doubting the shy child knew who he was or what he represented, he bent down, "and in my own crude way, and in my own graveled voice, I said, 'Caroline, in memory of your dear Papa, you kiss me.'" She did, to the cardinal's surprise.

The other iconic moment came from her brother. Like Caroline's kiss, John Junior's gesture came in response to an adult. As the soldiers again settled the president's casket onto the caisson, Mrs. Kennedy whispered into his ear that

The body bearers leaving the cathedral.

he could salute his daddy and say goodbye. The little boy loved pomp and color and uniforms. He promptly straightened to deliver a salute far more mature than his years, the best he had ever given.

Sergeant Pete Holder had turned the color team toward the boy "and I saw when he started to salute." So did millions of others there and on television. On the cathedral steps, White House correspondent Helen Thomas of the United Press shouted for her photographer to take the picture.

Six dozen still, motion-picture and television cameras across the street likewise captured the moment. It was the only frame one UPI man shot at St. Matthew's that day. Another image, taken from the side, captured a grim-faced Third Infantry captain delivering a textbook salute, with the boy in the blue coat behind him, innocently doing the same. Bishop Hannan was looking out over the street, toward the press and thousands of silent onlookers on the other side.

"When John John made that salute, they all burst into tears," he recalled. "Nobody got that picture. That picture would have been the quintessential weeping picture of the whole event."

Mrs. Kennedy, however, was gazing straight ahead and didn't see John's salute. Whether she had intended it for posterity or only for her son, the gesture left the watching world stricken. "You did it well, little man, you did it well," wrote a *Globe* columnist.

Even the troops struggled with their emotions. Adjutant Pond likened it to "the tragedy of combat: you can't stop and have time for emotion, you have to do what you have to do." Some didn't succeed. Sergeant Holder was over-whelmed by the casket and the realization that "the president of the United States was in there . . . I had to relieve myself from duty for a moment and take off my cap." The color sergeant was hardly alone. A widely reproduced news photo showed a sailor burying his face in gloved hands. Others remembered buddies who were similarly overcome. This wasn't the sort of duty anyone had ever drilled for.

From grief, the departure from St. Matthew's at one-thirty devolved almost into farce. One hundred seven vehicles waited on the narrow streets for the guests. Because of what the army history called "the mistaken, if well intended, intervention of a Presidential aide," only the family's limousines arrived in the correct order. Instead of the limousines for the heads of state, those for White House aides and staff pulled up next.

An unseemly scramble began. An Old Guard lieutenant later wrote that De Gaulle "was furious for being delayed and expressed his outrage to all within hearing." Most key dignitaries would arrive in time for the burial, but the tail

Old Guard troops in the procession.

of the caravan was just leaving St. Matthew's as the head reached Arlington. Some vehicles were packed, others nearly empty. Harry and Margaret Truman shared one car with Dwight and Mamie Eisenhower, while a sergeant representing the crew of Air Force One had another all to himself.

Again, the procession appeared more stately and perfect than it was. An off-duty air force weather officer knelt on the sidewalk beside his son and pointed out the passing dignitaries. It seemed, he recalled, "as if the entire United Nations passed by." Astronaut Colonel John Glenn went almost unnoticed.

The last vehicle was a ten-year-old blue Ford driven by Barney Ross, the president's old shipmate from PT-109. Their torpedo boat had been rammed and sunk by a Japanese destroyer in the Solomons one claustrophobic night in 1943. Now, Ross was taking two other survivors to Arlington for their skipper's burial.

Behind them, the capital was emptying as a million people headed home. "Stores were closed," reported *The Washington Post*. "Sidewalks were lonely. Traffic moved on tiptoe." But up ahead, said the *Daily News*, "the people at Arlington Cemetery waited in the cool, brisk, clear air. Hundreds had been waiting since early morning."

ARLINGTON

The procession, in Russell Baker's graceful phrase, was "a river of slowly moving uniforms." It flowed down Connecticut and Seventeenth to the national mall, onto Constitution and on around the Lincoln Memorial. The eight body bearers now marched flanking the caisson, with Bird behind and then Nemuth carrying the presidential flag.

The march to Arlington was "the saddest one of all," said *National Geographic,* "for now the numbness of initial shock had gone." As the caisson passed through what Nancy Dickerson called "a great stillness," people sometimes called out, as if to a listening spirit. A few said, "God bless you, Mr. President." Others simply spoke his name. The bands fell silent except for the drums as the troops swung onto Memorial Bridge between two enormous statues representing Valor and Sacrifice. Below, a few lonely anglers fished in the Potomac.

Waiting at Arlington was Jack Metzler. Like many of his generation, the cemetery superintendent was a veteran, an army sergeant in the war. He had served at the cemetery since 1951 and lived in a house on the grounds. His wife

The caisson and caravan approaching the cemetery.

and teenaged son stood now in the press area on the slope below the Custis-Lee mansion. As the marchers approached over the bridge, John Metzler, Jr. recognized the enormous stresses on his father.

"You look at all the movement to the cemetery," he recalled years later, after he had grown to manhood and assumed his father's old duties as superintendent, "and realize as it's coming across the bridge [that] all this becomes your responsibility once the remains get to the cemetery."

Banks of wreaths and bouquets covered the long treeless slope below the mansion. They came from the 2506 Cuban Brigade, the crew of the USS *Brazil*, the president and people of Israel, and many others. One with red, white and blue streamers read "Le General de Gaulle". Mrs. Kennedy had some of these flowers sent later to a children's home.

Journalists had received special credentials to stand together to the right of the massed flowers. Their pass was an ordinary cardboard tag that said ARLINGTON; a junior-high student could have counterfeited dozens. A *Newsday* photographer remembered having "to stand in place for a couple of hours and there was no respite from the cold. No going for coffee. No going to the rest room. If you left your place, it was gone." A group of nuns joined the press on the slope and after questioning by security men was allowed to stay.

The cemetery grounds were immaculate, as always. The slope had received extra attention and was meticulously raked and groomed. Yet in coming days, accounts of the burial often mentioned oak leaves swirling in the flawless blue sky. Some placed them at the beginning of the services, others nearer the end. A few noticed leaves rising on invisible currents, more remembered them fluttering down.

One newsman wondered if a vacuum created by the flyover had lifted the leaves into the air. The *Globe* reported they were dropped from a plane. But those who sensed the hand of God weren't alone.

"I'm not a religious person," the *Newsday* man recalled, "but maybe that day I was."

The Third Infantry from Fort Myer was stretched to exhaustion, but its officers worried mostly about other units. To compensate for other units' inexperience and inadequate rehearsals, the Old Guard had called on every available commissioned and noncommissioned officer of its own. These knowledgeable soldiers were to ensure that everyone turned at the right place and arrived in the proper position.

"Had these few remaining persons *not* been available," wrote Major Stanley P. Converse, executive officer of the first battalion and site control officer at Arlington, "I shudder to think what could have happened, particularly with those troops not trained in ceremonies."

Even so, the Old Guard had been forced to call for reinforcements. The secret service had greatly expanded the security cordon inside the cemetery on Sunday night and troops simply hadn't been available. A last-minute call to Fort Belvoir had brought an engineer battalion racing up to fill the gap. But it hadn't been in position when the gates opened, and civilian spectators had swept through, swamping the gravesite. Military police had spent hours shooing them back out.

At Mrs. Kennedy's request, the Fife and Drum Corps was formed opposite the bridge on a triangle of grass outside Memorial Gate. The musicians did not play, but remained at attention as the caisson passed, their colonial uniforms and wigs adding to the sad pageantry. The air force pipers and drummers were also in place inside the cemetery. They had arrived early that morning in their tartan kilts. "We rehearsed in our full outfits, and it was cold as hell," a drummer remembered.

There wasn't enough room for the whole procession in the cemetery. Only the cortege, the Marine Band and one platoon from each of the five services actually entered the grounds. The other units turned left before the gate and continued on to dismissal points where buses waited. None came for Lieutenant Oberg and the disappointed WAVES, who walked back to navy quarters near the Pentagon.

Old Guard troops in dress blues lined the narrow roads, presenting arms as the caisson passed by. Special forces troops in their green berets formed an honor cordon along a cocomat runner leading from the road up to the gravesite. The Irish Guard stood formed in two long lines near the

The body bearers climb the hillside.

grave. The air force pipers, bugler Keith Clark and the Old Guard's firing party and saluting battery were also in place. The Marine Band and the five platoons moved to assigned positions nearby.

Although it was two hours until sunset as the cortege approached, the hillside had already cast its shadow over the gravesite. Limousine drivers parked along the roadways and the dignitaries began walking in, some intermingling with the troops. The Marine Band played *Ruffles and Flourishes*, followed by the national anthem. The air force bagpipers slow-marched past the open grave playing *Mist Covered Mountain*; they would not play it again until gathered for a reunion thirty-nine years later. Mrs. Kennedy smiled faintly at the sound of the pipes. They were also the cue for the body bearers to unstrap and lift the casket from the caisson.

General Wehle led the color detail, cardinal and prelates, casket team, personal flag bearer and honor guard through the special forces' cordon and up the slope. Superintendent Metzler in a dark suit led the family forward, while secret service agents escorted the new president and his party. Twenty field-grade army officers in green winter uniforms and white gloves waited to escort the other dignitaries.

It was nearly three o'clock. The grays were breathing heavily and Bird and his men were weary. The lieutenant stepped aside to let Major Converse take command, but warned him that the team would need help carrying the casket up the hill to the gravesite. The major instructed Bird to stay with his men.

The distance from the caisson up the slope was about a hundred yards. The clergymen in front of the body bearers were so deliberate that the team nearly marched into them. New fears bubbled up inside them.

"I'm losing my grip, I'm losing my grip," one warned.

"Let go and grab it again," Sergeant Felder whispered back, "and I'll hold it up here." He interlocked his fingers around the casket handle and urged the others to do the same. With the weight and slow pace, the sergeant recalled, "it just felt like we were being pulled into the ground." He feared for a moment that they would have to set the casket down. Lieutenant Bird again stepped up to take some of the weight and help keep the team going.

Felder now realized that the unlit lamp for the eternal flame presented a new problem. Because of its location at the head of the grave, the body bearers had to carry the casket past the foot of the grave and then back it into place. To "back the casket on" meant changing their direction and grip without reversing the casket. This was "the last thing we wanted to do," Felder wrote. "But it had to be done and we did it."

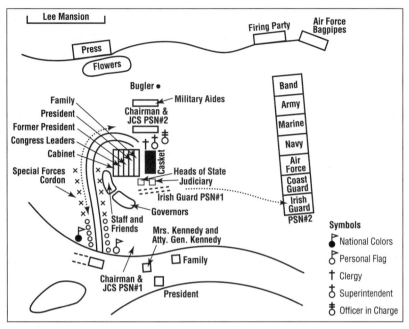

Participants positions at Arlington National Cemetery.

Twenty-six Irish cadets in their green and brown uniforms and cavalry boots delivered a rifle salute, hands perpendicular to their weapons. The eight body bearers turned and strained to settle the president's heavy casket atop its lowering device, a hard, awkward maneuver. If anything had gone wrong at that moment, Diamond said later, "we'd have jumped in the hole ourselves." The team then held the American flag tautly above the casket.

As Metzler escorted the family to their places, the first fighter-bombers appeared overhead. Mourners glanced up in surprise, but he had signaled them by radio ten minutes earlier. All other air traffic was grounded at nearby National.

The fifty aircraft represented each American state, thirty from the air force, twenty from the navy. They came from military bases in the south. The president had visited one of them, MacDill Air Force Base in Tampa, only four days before his death. Navy pilot Lieutenant Commander William P. Lawrence thought coordinating half a hundred jets from rival services in a tight airspace was "a nightmare." It looked perfect from below.

The formation arrived over Arlington in flights of three, in inverted V's, at four hundred miles an hour. The flights streaked above the cemetery one behind another, like arrows fired by skilled archers. Cloudbursts of noise cascaded from twenty-five hundred feet. Sixteen flights of three rushed past. Then came a seventeenth of two planes. This was the "missing man" formation, aviation's traditional salute for a lost airman.

Before many more months passed, squadrons of F-105 Thunderchiefs and F-4 Phantoms like these were engaged in a savage air war over Vietnam. Phantom pilot (later Vice Admiral) Lawrence was shot down and held captive in the north from 1967 to 1973.

The president's blue-and-white jetliner appeared over Arlington moments behind the fighters. It was designated SAM 26000 today because the commander-in-chief wasn't on board, but everyone still thought of it as Air Force One. Colonel Swindal swept above the hills at two thousand feet and dipped his wings before roaring away over Virginia. "The president liked the plane so much," he said later. "We just thought it would be nice to fly over." Across the river, watching from near the Washington Monument with his son, the off-duty air force weather officer saluted and broke into tears.

When the sky was again clear and quiet, the Irish Guard executed the silent drill that had moved the late president in Dublin. The cadets to the *Globe* were "the cream of a tiny military force in the land that has so many reasons to mourn him."

Their lieutenant issued his few commands before and after in Gaelic. The cadets presented their Enfield rifles at shoulder height, then slowly lowered them "until the muzzle rests on the ground in which the body is to be buried," the newspaper said. When they had finished, they moved off to stand beside the escort units.

Cardinal Cushing now commanded the solemn scene. He stepped up to the torch that awaited its flame, the world's leaders gathered behind him. The cardinal knew nothing about a military burial. He depended on a Catholic chaplain to guide him, "and from then on, I found out that I was on my own. And I did the best I could." Again using English rather than Latin, he delivered a prayer, followed by the Lord's Prayer and a blessing. He seemed almost to hurry, the *New York Times* said, "as if to end more quickly the anguish of Mrs. Kennedy and her family." With a final Amen, the gnarled old churchman stepped back.

Troops saluted as Captain Homer Gay's artillery battery then began firing to the southwest in McClellan Circle. Mrs. Kennedy seemed to flinch as the twenty-one echoes crashed off the hillsides. Not wanting to interrupt the military honors, the family decided to forgo planned readings of their own. When the cemetery was silent again, the cardinal pronounced the benediction. Uniformed troops presented arms as seven Third Infantry riflemen fired three quick volleys—a traditional signal from the Civil War, it meant that a burial party had completed its duties.

Now it was time for Taps. Sergeant Clark stood in the cold and the long shadows cradling his bugle. Officially, it was a Vincent Bach Corporation signal trumpet in B-flat, perhaps "the most elegant bugle ever made," according to music historians. Clark remembered a passage of scripture from 1 Corinthians:

*We shall all be changed, in a moment, in the twinkling of an
eye, at the last trumpet. For the trumpet shall sound, and the
dead shall be raised incorruptible, and we shall be changed.*

Although it sounded ancient, "Taps" had descended from
another call. Adapted by northern Brigadier General Daniel
Butterfield from "Tattoo" by Winfield Scott, it was first
sounded by bugler Oliver W. Norton during the Civil War.
The new call signaled "lights out" and soldiers called it "Go
to Sleep." But its twenty-four mournful notes were soon
sounded at military funerals in the Army of the Potomac.
Eventually, it spread to the Confederate army.

The call was "melancholy, yet full of rest and peace,"
Norton wrote after the war. "Its echoes linger in the heart
long after its tones have ceased to vibrate in the air." It had no
official lyrics and was rarely sung, but one verse was this:

*Day is done, gone the sun,
From the hills, from the lake,
From the sky.
All is well, safely rest,
God is nigh.*

Sergeant Clark turned his bugle toward Mrs. Kennedy.
Cold was the brass player's enemy, and he had stood out
here since morning. So that television might have a good
view, Major Converse had positioned his bugler too near
the firing party; Clark was now half deafened by the volleys. But he began perfectly, sounding the call only for the
widow, as he thought a good bugler must do. The notes
lingered in the air, audible a mile away.

Day is done, gone the sun . . .

He reached the sixth note and couldn't hold it. The cracked
note seemed born of emotion and somehow appropriate.
"The bugler's lip quivered for the nation," ABC's Edward

Bugler Keith C. Clark.

Morgan said later. The slip sounded so right, so exquisitely timed, that it became infectious—in coming weeks, other army buglers at Arlington mysteriously faltered at the same note. Elsewhere, lesser musicians tried to duplicate the mistake intentionally.

Clark didn't pause or falter. He sounded the remaining eighteen notes with pure, spare beauty; hearing the recording today can still bring shivers. The sergeant never excused his broken sixth note, saying he had missed it under pressure. No bugler in the world ever held it against him.

"When he cracked that note," recalled a high-school military academy bugler from New York, "I came to the sudden realization that everyone is mortal, even presidents and the best buglers."

As the Marine Band played the *Navy Hymn*, the body

The body bearers prepare to fold the flag.

bearers folded the flag "with whiplike precision," Tom Wicker wrote. Sergeant Felder checked that no red showed, then passed it down the line from man to man. Specialist Mayfield saluted and handed it to the superintendent. Cardinal Cushing delivered what he later called an "extemporaneous blessing" for the eternal flame as the band finished the hymn, then Superintendent Metzler quietly presented the flag to the president's widow. Cameras captured her anguish through her veil as she clutched the triangular blue bundle with its white stars.

Major Converse, graying and ruggedly handsome in his blues, lighted a long taper, which he handed to Mrs. Kennedy. "This is the saddest moment of my life," he said.

Converse guided her hand as she touched the taper to the plain black lamp and ignited the eternal flame. Robert and Ted Kennedy then each held the taper to the lamp, although the flame was already dancing. The veiled widow standing with the last brothers, historian Theodore White wrote, "made a group atavism, calling to the blood, an echo of tribal life of primitive Gaels and Celts before Christianity gentled them."

The end of the service, said a White House advisor, was "like the fall of a curtain, or the snapping of taut strings." Mrs. Kennedy shook hands with the Cardinal and the prelates before turning to leave with her family. She paused only to embrace General Maxwell Taylor, her husband's friend, an old hero he had summoned from retirement to lead the joint chiefs. "Then, after that moment of emotion," said the *New York Times*, "she resolutely took Robert Kennedy's hand and filed out through the line of soldiers."

John Connally III, seventeen-year-old son of the Texas governor, had been standing beside President Johnson and his party. He had a note in his pocket from his mother to the former first lady. The president took young Connally down the hillside and introduced him to the attorney general and Mrs. Kennedy. She took the teenager's hand.

"I hope you'll tell your mother that I'm so glad your father will be okay," she said. "That's the only good thing to come out of this."

Then Mrs. Kennedy returned to the White House to greet the many foreign visitors. "It would be most ungracious of me," she said, "not to have all those people in our house."

The troops hadn't rehearsed leaving the gravesite. A staff officer asked Lieutenant Colonel Cross what to do. The Old Guard commander ordered a right face, forward march at trail arms to climb the hill toward the mansion. The troops and bands all left that way to be transported back to their various barracks. The body bearers, however, remained in formation as mourners began filing slowly past the grave.

Marine Jerry Diamond had been so focused on his duties beside the casket that he only now noticed the crowd. The size of it awed him. "We stood there and stood there and stood there," Staff Sergeant Gaudreau remembered. "The lieutenant was waiting for all these people to leave. It seemed like it would never end."

When the time came to go, Bird marched his men down the slope, halted them and ordered an about-face. There for the last time he broke protocol, ordering a last, private hand salute to the late president. They had been with him so long, Bird told historian Manchester, and felt such emotion, that "we just wanted to do it." With that, their duty ended. Sergeant Felder left the cemetery feeling "terribly empty."

The special forces were equally reluctant to leave. They, too, did something extraordinary, and posted their own honor guard. A soldier with rifle and fixed bayonet remained at each corner of the grave until the contingent had to depart for Fort Bragg. Before they left, Command Sergeant Major Ruddy placed a green beret near the eternal flame.

Colonel Grieves said later that he had borrowed a custom from the Greek raiding forces. If the president could overrule the army to let the special forces don their green berets, Grieves added, "We could at least give one back." The First Special Forces Group (Airborne) would later add a permanent black border to its yellow "flash," the unit patch worn on the headgear. When the green berets left the grave, Lieutenant Colonel Cross, Major Converse, another officer and the command sergeant major briefly replaced them.

Other troops soon noticed Ruddy's gesture. A military policeman left his brassard. An Old Guard soldier added his buff strap and a brass unit insignia called a cockade to the evergreen boughs surrounding the lamp. After images of the beret appeared on television and in newspapers, the other branches followed what became an instant tradition. For the next several years, until a permanent site was constructed, fresh military caps always decorated the grave.

None of this appeared on Monday's telecasts. The pool camera kept broadcasting live images as workers prepared to lower the casket, so Superintendent Metzler cut electricity to the entire post. "I saw no reason why the ghouls should be making a picture of that," he said later.

The president was quietly interred at three thirty-two as evening descended on Washington. It was the twenty-fourth and last burial of the day at Arlington.

EPILOGUE

EPILOGUE

The Fife and Drum Corps was back in its barracks when the artillery began firing again that evening. A fifty-gun salute traditionally followed the lowering of the flag on the day of a president's funeral. The only other day fifty guns were fired was the Fourth of July. At Fort Myer, the Old Guard salute battery fired every five seconds for more than four minutes.

Boom! . . . Boom! . . . Boom! . . . Boom!

"We just looked at each other in silence and shook our heads," drummer Bob Parker said half a lifetime later.

Seventy-two hours of duty and bleak pageantry began taking a toll. Some troops who had worked on emotional autopilot now broke down at unexpected moments. Others who had focused with almost blinkered intensity remembered small details more than the sweeping tableaus. Sam Bird sat in his quarters with a tape recorder to capture his memories. Jim Felder went home to his wife and baby in their off-base apartment, then burst into tears while watching the television news.

The next few years proved difficult.

Captain Mike Groves didn't reach the war in Vietnam. On the Tuesday night following Thanksgiving, eight days after the president's funeral, media officer Eugene Bickley was on duty at MDW headquarters. Another officer called to inform him that Groves had died of a heart attack while dining with his family in their quarters at Fort Myer. He was twenty-seven years old.

A congressman said in the House of Representatives the next day that the captain had overtaxed himself during the funeral and that his death was "another tragic incident" flowing from the assassination. The Old Guard later named a barracks in Groves' honor.

Sergeant Felder was on leave when he learned of the death of his friend and captain. "I want you to do his funeral," Groves' widow said. "He would have wanted it that way." On Friday, December 6, Jim Felder, Sam Bird and the caisson team escorted Mike Groves' body to burial not far from President Kennedy. Afterwards, Felder turned in his gear and said it was his last funeral at Arlington. He never worked another.

Felder left the Old Guard six weeks later at the end of his army obligation, returned to South Carolina and entered law school. In 1970, he was among the first African Americans since Reconstruction to be elected to the state legislature.

Sam Bird was promoted to captain and company commander in the Old Guard. In 1966, he was assigned to the First Cavalry Division (Airmobile) in South Vietnam. A junior officer who met him outside An Khe recalled that "you could still see the shine on his boot tips beneath the road dust."

Bird excelled as a combat leader and asked to extend his

stay with his company. On January 27, 1967, his twenty-seventh birthday, enemy small-arms fire struck him in the head and legs. The head wound was not unlike the president's. A lieutenant used his hands to keep Bird's brains inside his skull. The helicopter pilot who flew him out wondered why he was "risking my crew for a dead man."

The captain somehow survived but was disabled, confined to a wheelchair and later retired. In a ceremony at his bedside, a brigadier general awarded him two bronze stars, the purple heart and an air medal. Senator Robert Kennedy learned of Bird's condition and sent him a warm letter. He added a handwritten postscript: "Mrs. John Kennedy also asked to be remembered to you."

Bird returned to Kansas, where he married a childhood friend and maintained close ties with the army and the Citadel. For years his health deteriorated. He died on October 18, 1984, more than seventeen years after his wounding, and was buried in Wichita.

In 1988, thanks to efforts by veterans groups and Senator Robert Dole, Bird's name was added to the black granite wall at the Vietnam Veterans Memorial. His widow later wrote his biography.

Lieutenant Bickley followed Bird to South Vietnam in 1967. On his twenty-sixth day in country, Bickley, too, was seriously wounded, by an exploding landmine. Unlike Bird, he recovered and remained in the army. In 1974, then a major, he wrote an article for an army magazine describing the duties that he, Sam Bird and Mike Groves had performed in November 1963.

Sergeant Keith Clark retired from the army in 1966 after twenty years in uniform. He said that missing a note during a performance could happen to anyone, but added, "You never really get over it."

Clark enjoyed a successful second career as a performer, teacher and writer before his death in 2002 at age seventy-four. He, too, was buried in Arlington. The cemetery's historian later observed that the cracked sixth note "showed the tension that the nation felt. . . . It's what should happen. And in that way, it almost personalized it. And it made it immortal."

Several others servicemen and bandsmen also became newsworthy. Hometown and military journalists often asked them for interviews on anniversaries of the assassination and funeral. The veterans got accustomed to identifying themselves in film and photos of the funeral. "I've seen it a thousand times," retired Senior Master Sergeant Richard Gaudreau said, "and I'll see it another thousand times."

Nine days after the president's funeral, Patrick Kennedy and an unnamed, stillborn daughter were quietly re-interred beside their father in the national cemetery. A permanent memorial site was later completed a few yards from the original. A contingent from the U.S. Army Band played hymns during an unannounced dedication on March 15, 1967.

"Be at peace, dear Jack, with your tiny infants by your side, until we all meet again above this hill and beyond the stars," Cardinal Cushing said that rainy morning. Senator Robert Kennedy was buried nearby after his assassination in June 1968.

Mrs. Kennedy, who had married and divorced shipping magnate Aristotle Onassis, died in May 1994 and was buried beside the president and their infants. "During those four endless days in 1963, she held us together as a family and a country," Senator Edward Kennedy said in his eulogy. "In large part because of her, we could grieve and then go on."

After leaving the cemetery on that gloomy Thanksgiving Day in 1963, Mrs. Kennedy and her children had flown on an air force jet to Massachusetts. There in an interview with Theodore White at the family compound at Hyannis Port, she first likened her husband's White House to a popular Broadway musical.

It may not have occurred to her that in its final scenes, she had delivered *Camelot's* finest performance. As *The London Evening Standard* famously observed following the president's funeral, "Jacqueline Kennedy has given the American people from this day on one thing they have always lacked—majesty."

APPENDICES

FUNERAL ORDER OF MARCH

MONDAY, NOVEMBER 25, 1963

Lead

Police escort (5)

Escort commander (1)

Commander of troops (6)

First march unit

Marine Band (91)

Military Academy, company (89)

Naval Academy, company (89)

Air Force Academy, company (89)

Coast Guard Academy, company (89)

Army, 3rd Infantry (Old Guard), company (89)

Navy, Potomac River Naval Command, company (89)

Air Force, 11th Wing, Bolling AFB, squadron, (89)

Coast Guard, Baltimore District, company (89)

Servicewomen, composite, company (82)

Second march unit

Navy Band (91)

Army National Guard, 116th MP Battalion, D.C.,
company (89)

Army Reserve, 317th Regiment, 80th Division,
company (89)

Marine Corps Reserve, 13th Battalion, company (89)

Navy Reserve, Naval Air Facility Andrews, company (89)

Air National Guard, Andrews AFB, squadron (89)

Air Force Reserve, Andrews AFB, squadron (89)

Coast Guard Reserve, Cape May, N.J., company (89)

Third march unit

Air Force Band (91)

Representatives, veterans' organizations

Army Special Forces, Fort Bragg, N.C., platoon (38)

Marine Corps, Marine Barracks, company (89)

Cortege

Special honor guard (Joint Chiefs)

National color detail

Clergy

Caisson and body bearers

Personal flag bearer

Caparisoned horse

Kennedy family

Rear

Police escort

Flyover

(50 aircraft)

4th Fighter Wing, Seymour Johnson AFB, N.C.

Fighter Squadron 14, NAS Cecil Field, Fla.

4453rd Combat Crew Training Squadron, MacDill AFB, Fla.

NOTABLE PARTICIPANTS
MONDAY, NOVEMBER 25, 1963

Troop Commanders
Major General Philip C. Wehle, USA
Military District of Washington

Lieutenant Colonel Richard E. Cross, USA
Third U.S. Infantry

Captain Michael D. Groves, USA
Honor Guard Company

First Lieutenant Samuel R. Bird, USA
Body Bearers

Color Guard
Sergeant James R. Holder, USA
Airman Third Class Kenneth L. Freeman, USAF
Lance Corporal Harold M. Moffett, USMC

Caisson Team

Sergeant Thomas M. Satterberg, USA

Specialist Fourth Class Charles B. Wade, USA

Private First Class James P. Stimpson, USA

Private First Class Richard A. Pace, USA

Body Bearers

Sergeant James L. Felder, USA

Specialist Fourth Class Douglas A. Mayfield, USA

Lance Corporal Timothy F. Cheek, USMC

Private First Class Jerry J. Diamond, USMC

Seaman Apprentice Hubert Clark, USN

Seaman Apprentice Larry B. Smith, USN

Staff Sergeant Richard E. Gaudreau, USAF

Yeoman Second Class George A. Barnum, USCG

Presidential Standard Bearer

Seaman Apprentice Edward W. Nemuth, USN

Bugler

Specialist Sixth Class Keith Clark, USA

Horses

Big Boy (lead); Skyline and Count Chris (lead team);
Blue Dare and Blue (swing team); Cap and Cloudburst
(wheel team); Black Jack (caparisoned)

MUSICAL SELECTIONS

MONDAY, NOVEMBER 25, 1963
PROCESSION, MASS AND BURIAL

Coast Guard Academy Band, Capitol Plaza

Ruffles and Flourishes

Hail to the Chief

O God of Loveliness

Marine Band, march to White House

Our Fallen Heroes

Holy, Holy, Holy

The Vanished Army

Navy Band, march to White House

Beethoven Funeral March

R. B. Hall Funeral March

Onward Christian Soldiers

Air Force Band, march to White House

Chopin Funeral March

Vigor in Arduis (Hymn to the Holy Name)

America the Beautiful

Naval Academy Catholic Choir, White House

Above the Hills of Time the Cross Is Gleaming
(Londonderry Air)

Eternal Father, Strong to Save
(Navy Hymn)

Dona Nobis Pacem

Black Watch (Royal Highland), March to
St. Matthew's

The Brown Haired Maiden

The Badge of Scotland

The 51st Highland Division

The Barren Rocks of Aden

Army Band, St. Matthew's

Ruffles and Flourishes

Hail to the Chief

Pray for the Dead

St. Matthew's Choir, tenor soloist Luigi Vena

Subvenite (choir)

Pie Jesu, Leybach (soloist)

Ave Maria, Schubert (soloist)

In Manus Tuus, Novello (soloist)

Sanctus and Benedictus, Perosi (choir)

Agnus Dei, Bizet (soloist)

In Paradisum (choir)

Army Band, St. Matthew's

Ruffles and Flourishes

Hail to the Chief

Holy God, We Praise Thy Name

Service bands, March to Arlington National Cemetery

Same as from Capitol to White House

Marine Band, Arlington

Ruffles and Flourishes

The Star Spangled Banner

Air Force Pipe Band, Arlington

Mist Covered Mountain

Army bugler, Arlington

Taps

Marine Band, Arlington

Eternal Father, Strong to Save (Navy Hymn)

ACKNOWLEDGMENTS

Many thanks to my brother Jon Leeke, a sergeant in the Third U.S. Infantry during the Reagan administration, for long ago relating Old Guard barracks lore that turned out to be true. Thanks, too, to Bill Tabor and Elise Fulstone for spotting this book in yet another idea and escorting it to publication.

For their recollections of November 1963, I am very grateful to Richard Gaudreau, Jerry Diamond, Jo Oberg, Gilbert Mitchell, Vincent Battista, James Robertson, Jr. and John Bruneel, Sr. For other assistance, my thanks to Kirk Heflin of The Old Guard Museum, Master Sergeant Michael Yoder of the U.S. Army Band, and various other military historians and presidential archivists. Any factual errors are the author's.

William Manchester's *The Death of a President* is indispensable to understanding the funeral of President Kennedy. B. C. Mossman's and M. W. Stark's *The Last Salute*, published by the Department of the Army, is equally valuable.

SELECT
BIBLIOGRAPHY

BOOKS

Associated Press. *The Torch Is Passed: The Associated Press Story of the Death of a President*. New York,1963.

Berry, Wendell, and Ben Shahn (ill.). *November Twenty Six Nineteen Hundred Sixty Three*. New York, 1964.

Bigler, Philip. *In Honored Glory: Arlington National Cemetery; The Final Post*. Clearwater, 1999.

Bird, Annette and Tim Prouty. *So Proudly He Served: The Sam Bird Story*. Wichita, 1993.

Bishop, Jim. *The Day Kennedy Was Shot*. New York, 1968.

Breslin, Jimmy. *The World of Jimmy Breslin*. New York, 1967.

Dallas Morning News. *November 22: The Day Remembered, As Reported by* The Dallas Morning News. Dallas, 1990.

Dockery, Martin J. *Lost in Translation: Vietnam: A Combat Advisor's Story*. New York, 2003.

Felder, James L. *I Buried John F. Kennedy*. Columbia, 1994.

Lawrence, William P., and Rosario Rausa. *Tennessee Patriot: The Naval Career of Vice Admiral William P. Lawrence, U.S. Navy*. Annapolis, 2006.

Lubin, David M. *Shooting Kennedy: JFK and the Culture of Images*. Berkeley, 2003.

Manchester, William. *The Death of a President, November 20–November 25, 1963*. New York, 1967.

Mossman, B. C., and M. W. Stark. *The Last Salute: Civil and Military Funerals, 1921–1969*. Washington, 1971.

National Broadcasting Company. *Seventy Hours and Thirty Minutes*. New York, 1966.

Osterhaus, Joe. *Radiance*. Lincoln, 2002.

Proffitt, Nicholas. *Gardens of Stone*. New York, 1983.

Schneider, Richard H. *Taps: Notes from a Nation's Heart*. New York, 2002.

Semple, Robert B., Jr., ed. *Four Days in November: The Original Coverage of the John F. Kennedy Assassination by the Staff of the* New York Times. New York, 2003.

Trost, Cathy, and Susan Bennett, eds. *President Kennedy Has Been Shot: The Inside Story of the Murder of a President*. Naperville, 2003.

United Press International. *Four Days: The Historical Record of the Death of President Kennedy, Compiled by United Press International and* American Heritage *Magazine*. New York, 1964.

White, Theodore H. *The Making of the President 1964*. New York, 1965.

Print Articles

Bickley, Eugene H. "Memories of the JFK Funeral." *Soldiers* November 1974, 48–51.

Britton, Bob. "Former Presidio Commander Remembers President Kennedy's Funeral in 1963." *Globe* (Defense Language Institute Foreign Language Center, Presidio of Monterey). November 1997, 20–23.

Collins, B. T. "The Courage of Sam Bird." *Reader's Digest.* May 1989, 49–54.

Cooney, Terence P. "Sunday at the White House." *Armor.* November—December, 1966, 43–46.

Darcy, James. "Vets Share Stories of Old Guard's Most-public Hour." *Pentagram.* December 18, 1998.

Giffels, David. "Carrying JFK Then and Now," *Akron (Ohio) Beacon-Journal.* November 20, 2003.

Hartman, Brenda. "Assigned a Role in History." *Bloomsburg (PA) Press Enterprise.* November 22, 2003.

Leaning, John. "Still Standing at Attention: Orleans Man Recalls Serving on Honor Guard at President's Funeral." *Cape Cod Times.* November 22, 2003.

Paschall, Rod. "The Armed Forces and the Assassination." *American History.* December 2003, 55–56.

Preston, Tim. "Vivid Memories of the Day JFK Died," *Sanford (North Carolina) Herald.* November 21, 2003.

Tuchman, Barbara W. "Outpouring of Foreign Dignitaries a Tribute to Position of U.S. and to Its Late President." *St. Louis Post-Dispatch.* November 26, 1963.

Tudor, Jason. "The Pipes are Calling: Bandsmen Blow, Squeeze and Wiggle Their Way into Tiny Fraternity Marked by Historical Significance," *Citizen Airman*. December 2004, 8–11.

Villanueva, Jari. "The 40th Anniversary of The Broken Note." *Washington Post*. November 23, 2003.

ONLINE ARTICLES

———. "Corps Built Kennedy's Eternal Flame." *Engineer Update*. November 2003. Available at www.hq.usace. army.mil. Accessed April 18, 2005.

———. "Visitor Information, Monuments and Memorials: President John Fitzgerald Kennedy." Arlington National Cemetery Web site. Available at www.arlingtoncemetery. org. Accessed April 28, 2005.

Military Historical Society of Minnesota. "Third United States Infantry: 'The Old Guard.'" Available at www. dma.state.mn.us. Accessed October 6, 2005.

Miller, John C. "John F. Kennedy's Visit to the Barracks." Center House Association. Available at www.centerhouse. org. Accessed April 18, 2005.

Villanueva, Jari. "The 11th Wing and the Kennedy Funeral." *The Beam*. Bolling Air Force Base. November 28, 2003. Available at www.jvmusic.net. Accessed April 17, 2005.

———. "24 Notes That Tap Deep Emotions." Available at www.west-point.org/taps/Taps.html. Accessed July 1, 2005.

Manuscripts, interviews, and papers:

Battista, Vincent. telephone interview by author. November 7, 2005.

Bird, Samuel R. "After Action Report, Joint Casket Team – State Funeral, President John Fitzgerald Kennedy," December 10, 1963. Courtesy of Richard E. Gaudreau. Also available at the Old Guard Museum archives.

Bruneel, John B., Sr. email to author. October 24 and 25, 2005.

Chiarodo, Marie. "Marie Fehmer Chiarodo Oral History Interview II." Transcript dated August 16, 1972, by Joe B. Frantz. Internet copy, LBJ Library and Museum.

Converse, Stanley P. "After Action Report, President Kennedy Funeral (Interment Ceremony)." December 17, 1963. The Old Guard Museum archives.

Diamond, Jerry J. email to author. September 29, 2005.

———. telephone interview by author. October 31, 2005.

Gaudreau, Richard E. email to author. September 30, October 4 and 10, 2005.

Lipsey, Richard A. "HSCA Interview With Richard Lipsey, 1-18-78." Transcript by Debra Conway, JFK Lancer Productions and Publications. Available online at www.historymatters.com. Accessed April 21, 2005.

Miller, Paul C. "After Action Report – President John F. Kennedy's Funeral." November 26, 1963. Available at www.jfklibrary.org. Accessed March 7, 2007.

Mitchell, Gilbert H. telephone interview by author. November 7, 2005.

Oberg, Jo. letter to author. May 24, 2006.

——. "A Christmas Letter, 1963: Lieutenant Commander Jo Oberg, US Navy (Ret.) and President Kennedy's Assassination." History and Collections, Women in Military Service for America Memorial, Inc. Courtesy of Jo Oberg. Also available at www.womensmemorial.org. Accessed October 28, 2005.

Parker, Robert. "Bob Parker: A Different Drummer." Interview by Carlos R. Guzman. Available at www. ludwigdrummer.com; also as "The Memories of Robert Parker: 1962–1964" at http://ogfdc.org. Accessed April 17, 2005.

Robertson, James I. Jr. email to author. July 14, 2005.

Wilson, Walter. "Engineer Memoirs: Lieutenant General Walter K. Wilson, Jr." Available at www.usace.army.mil. Accessed April 18, 2005.

NEWSPAPERS AND PERIODICALS

Bolling (Air Force Base) Beam

Boston Globe

Chicago Daily News

Dallas Morning News

Life

Look

National Geographic

New York Times

Newsweek

Pentagram

St. Louis Post-Dispatch

Soldiers

Time

The Times (London)

Washington Daily News

The Washington Post

Washington Evening Star

VIDEO

Drew, Robert. *Faces of November*. Bonus film with *Crisis: Behind a Presidential Commitment*. 12 min. Drew Associates. 1963, 1991. DVD.

Wolper, David L. *Four Days in November*. Produced and directed by Mel Stuart. 122 min. United Artists. 1964. Videocassette.

INDEX

Page numbers in *italics* refer to illustrations.

Attic Window Publishing, Inc., Washington, DC's local interest publisher, produces quality non-fiction books about the region's history and guides to enjoying the best the area has to offer. Comments about this book and author inquiries may be emailed to atticwindow@earthlink.net or mailed to the publisher at 4905 Maury Lane, Alexandria, VA 22304.